The Critical Idiom

Founder Editor: **John D. Jump (1969–1976)**

2 Romanticism

A, 2-25

In the same series

Romanticism/*Lilian R. Furst*

Methuen

LONDON and NEW YORK

First published 1969
by Methuen & Co. Ltd
11 New Fetter Lane, London EC4P 4EE
Second edition 1976
Reprinted twice
Reprinted 1982

Published in the USA by
Methuen & Co.
in association with Methuen, Inc.
733 Third Avenue, New York, NY 10017

Printed in Great Britain at the
University Press, Cambridge

ISBN 0 416 83910 X (Hardback)
ISBN 0 416 83920 7 (Paperback)

Contents

Contents

Founder Editor's Preface

The volumes composing the Critical Idiom deal with a wide variety of key terms in our critical vocabulary. The purpose of the series differs from that served by the standard glossaries of literary terms. Many terms are adequately defined for the needs of students by the brief entries in these glossaries, and such terms do not call for attention in the present series. But there are other terms which cannot be made familiar by means of compact definitions. Students need to grow accustomed to them through simple and straightforward but reasonably full discussions. The purpose of this series is to provide such discussions.

Many critics have borrowed methods and criteria from currently influential bodies of knowledge or belief that have developed without particular reference to literature. In our own century, some of them have drawn on art-history, psychology, or sociology. Others, strong in a comprehensive faith, have looked at literature from a Marxist or a Christian or some other sharply defined point of view. The result has been the importation into literary criticism of terms from the vocabularies of these sciences and creeds. Discussions of such bodies of knowledge and belief in their bearing upon literature and literary criticism form a natural extension of the initial aim of the Critical Idiom.

Because of their diversity of subject-matter, the studies in the series vary considerably in structure. But all the authors have tried to give as full illustrative quotation as possible, to make reference whenever appropriate to more than one literature, and to write in such a way as to guide readers towards the short bibliographies in which they have made suggestions for further reading.

John D. Jump

University of Manchester

Acknowledgements

I should like to express my thanks to Professor J. D. Jump for his sound and ready advice at every stage as well as for the helpful suggestions of his editorial pencil. I am also most grateful to four research students, Miss J. Aldridge, Miss B. Blades, Mrs M. Gluckman and Miss C. Robinson for their meticulous scrutiny of the typescript and for their constructive criticisms.

In preparing the second revised edition I must acknowledge the help of many students who have used the first edition, have asked questions and made comments which have revealed to me new aspects of Romanticism as well as gaps in my text. I am specially indebted to my colleague Dr Robert M. Jackson, and to Antonio Gil, William Sims, Janet Sutherland and Dr Ester Zago, graduate students at the University of Oregon, for helpful suggestions and bibliographical information. And last but by no means least to Pat Krier for coping with my scribbles with such understanding and goodwill.

1

Definitions and usage

Post-Romantic usage

'He who seeks to define Romanticism is entering a hazardous occupation which has claimed many victims.' This timely warning was issued by E. B. Burgum in an article on Romanticism in the *Kenyon Review* of 1941, but it has not deterred critics in their ceaseless endeavours to arrive at some definition of this term. The definitions are, therefore, legion, numbering almost as many as those who have written on this subject. The difficulty in approaching Romanticism is thus less that of of finding *a* definition, than of finding one's way through the maze of definitions that have already been put forward. The aim of this monograph is not to add one more to the list of definitions under the illusion that it may be *the* right one; but rather to explore the origins and manifestations of the literary movement of the early nineteenth century known as Romanticism in the hope of achieving some clearer picture of the kind of writing to which this term is applied.

The bewildering variety of definitions and meanings and the sense of dissatisfaction with them have long given rise to complaint. In 1923, for instance, Grierson wrote that Romantic, like Classical, was a term 'no attempt to define which ever seems entirely convincing to oneself or to others' (*Background of English Literature*, p. 256). Lovejoy, a year later, was far more emphatic: 'The word "romantic" has come to mean so many things that, by itself, it means nothing. It has ceased to perform the functions of a verbal sign' (Lovejoy, 'On the Discriminations of Romanticisms', *English Romantic Poets*,

p. 6). Lovejoy's contention is admirably illustrated by Barzun's 'sampling of modern usage' in Chapter X of *Classic, Romantic and Modern*, where he cites examples of the word being used as a synonym for the following adjectives: 'attractive', 'unselfish', 'exuberant', 'ornamental', 'unreal', 'realistic', 'irrational', 'materialistic', 'futile', 'heroic', 'mysterious and soulful', 'noteworthy', 'conservative', 'revolutionary', 'bombastic', 'picturesque', 'nordic', 'formless', 'formalistic', 'emotional', 'fanciful', 'stupid'. No wonder that the term has been dismissed as no more than an 'approximate label', a 'serviceable makeshift' (M. Praz, *The Romantic Agony*, p. 21) that we cannot do without, but cannot hope ever to pin down to a precise meaning.

This discouraging view would seem to be confirmed by the incongruous assortment of definitions that have been evolved in the last hundred and fifty years. A fair cross-section of these has been gathered by E. Bernbaum in *Guide through the Romantic Movement*, pp. 301–2, and it is worth quoting because it shows the extraordinary range of senses that have been attributed to this term:

Romanticism is disease, Classicism is health. GOETHE.

A movement to honour whatever Classicism rejected. Classicism is the regularity of good sense, – perfection in moderation; Romanticism is disorder in the imagination, – the rage of incorrectness. A blind wave of literary egotism. BRUNETIÈRE.

Classic art portrays the finite, romantic art also suggests the infinite. HEINE.

The illusion of beholding the infinite within the stream of nature itself, instead of apart from that stream. MORE.

A desire to find the infinite within the finite, to effect a synthesis of the real and the unreal. The expression in art of what in theology would be called pantheistic enthusiasm. FAIRCHILD.

The return to nature. ROUSSEAU.

In general a thing is romantic when, as Aristotle would say, it is wonderful rather than probable; in other words, when it violates the normal sequence of cause and effect in favour of adventure. The whole movement is filled with the praise of ignorance, and of those who still enjoy its inappreciable advantages, – the savage, the peasant, and above all the child. BABBITT.

The opposite, not of Classicism, but of Realism, – a withdrawal from outer experience to concentrate upon inner. ABERCROMBIE.

Liberalism in literature. Mingling the grotesque with the tragic or sublime (forbidden by classicism); the complete truth of life. VICTOR HUGO.

The re-awakening of the life and thought of the Middle Ages. HEINE.

The cult of the extinct. GEOFFREY SCOTT.

The classic temper studies the past, the romantic neglects it. SCHELLING.

An effort to escape from actuality. WATERHOUSE.

Sentimental melancholy. PHELPS.

Vague aspiration. PHELPS.

Subjectivity, the love of the picturesque, and a reactionary spirit [against whatever immediately preceded it]. PHELPS.

Romanticism is, at any time, the art of the day; Classicism, the art of the day before. STENDHAL.

Emotion rather than reason; the heart opposed to the

head. GEORGE SAND.

A liberation of the less conscious levels of the mind; an intoxicating dreaming. Classicism is control by the conscious mind. LUCAS.

Imagination as contrasted with reason and the sense of fact. NEILSON.

Extraordinary development of imaginative sensibility. HERFORD.

An accentuated predominance of emotional life, provoked or directed by the exercise of imaginative vision, and in its turn stimulating or directing such exercise. CAZAMIAN.

The renascence of wonder. WATTS-DUNTON.

The addition of strangeness to beauty. PATER.

The fairy way of writing. KER.

The spirit counts for more than the form. GRIERSON.

Whereas in classical works the idea is represented directly and with as exact an adaptation of form as possible, in romantic the idea is left to the reader's faculty of divination assisted only by suggestion and symbol. SAINTSBURY.

Moreover, new and increasingly sophisticated definitions could be added each year: in a series of recent talks on the sources of Romanticism Isaiah Berlin summarized its essence as 'the tyranny of art over life', while Wellek conceives it as compounded of a particular view of imagination, a particular attitude to nature and a particular use of symbols.

The confusion has become so great that a separate sub-species has arisen which seeks to review the existent definitions and as far as possible to categorize them: those that distinguish primarily between 'romantic' and 'classical', those that oppose 'romantic' to 'realistic', those that separate 'intrinsic' from 'historic' Romanticism, those formulated by the pro-Romantics and those of the anti-Romantics, etc. For practical purposes, however, it proves more helpful to recognize the difference between those definitions that are of an inclusive nature and those, on the contrary, that tend to the restrictive. The former type is exemplified in Bernbaum's list by the phrases of Goethe, Stendhal, Babbitt, Heine, Fairchild or by the purely descriptive neutral approach of a sentence such as Thorlby's: 'The adjective "romantic" is commonly applied to various artistic styles and works, some philosophical writing, occasionally also manners and dress, which made their appearance in Europe between about 1770 and 1830,' (*The Romantic Movement*, p.1). These comprehensive definitions are in fact too wide to form a viable working basis. Used in this way, the word 'romantic' has as little or as much meaning as 'conservative' in politics and it can be so ingeniously and arbitrarily extended as to become virtually useless as a term of literary criticism. At the other extreme, the restrictive definitions, such as those of Geoffrey Scott, Pater and Phelps, certainly had the advantage of sharpness, but they are so narrow that they will in practice inevitably involve the critic in constant and agonizing debates as to whether poet X or novelist Y is, strictly speaking, a Romantic or not. There is also a more serious objection to this kind of definition, which has been pointed out by Babbitt:

A fruitful source of false definition is to take as primary in a more or less closely allied group of facts what is actually secondary – for example, to fix upon the return to the Middle Ages as the central fact in romanticism, whereas this return is only symptomatic; it is very far from being the original phenomenon. Confused and incomplete definitions of romanticism have indeed just that origin – they seek to put at the centre something that though romantic is not central but peripheral, and so the whole subject is thrown out of perspective.

(I. Babbitt, *Rousseau and Romanticism*, pp. 2–3)

'Confused and incomplete', narrow and restrictive such definitions may well be, but to brand them *ipso facto* as 'false' is unwarranted. This indeed is one of the sources of difficulty: that none of the definitions offered, either the inclusive or the restrictive, seems absolutely wrong inasmuch as each could be justified by reference to certain works or views. Conversely, none seems totally right and finally satisfying in so far as there are always exceptions and problems, whichever one is accepted as the best – or the least bad.

The roots of this impasse lie not so much in any defects on the part of the aspiring definers as in the character of the Romantic movement itself. For this staggering array of possible definitions only reflects a salient quality of European Romanticism: its innate complexity and multiplicity. An artistic movement as deep, as many-faceted, and, incidentally, as long-lived as Romanticism had to manifest itself in any number of directions, and it is fundamentally this that confounds the task of definition. To try to seize Romanticism in its entirety in a neat catch-phrase is an endeavour as doomed to failure as it is futile. We must in this instance reverse the usual order by seeking to understand Romanticism as a phenomenon before attempting to catch it in the net of definition.

The Romantics' own usage

These problems of definition and inconsistencies of usage are by no means confined solely to the twentieth century; many of those poets and thinkers of the late eighteenth and early nineteenth centuries whom we generally regard as Romantics were themselves perplexed by this word. Some were also quite unscrupulous in the uses they made of the term 'romantic', which they interpreted very freely to suit their own purposes, as their statements reveal.

No one was more erratic in this than the brilliant but mercurial Friedrich Schlegel, who is usually held responsible for introducing the word into the literary context. In spite of his boast in 1797 that he had written some 125 pages in explanation of the term, he does not appear ever to have arrived at any single, let alone definitive meaning, and there can be no doubt that his writings are a fertile source of muddle and misunderstanding. Throughout his theoretical pronouncements the connotation of 'romantisch' fluctuates disconcertingly, not only from work to work, but even within the limits of one and the same work. While his brother August Wilhelm, of a more orderly turn of mind, used the word fairly consistently in both the *Vorlesungen über schöne Literatur und Kunst (Lectures on 'belles-lettres' and art)* and the *Vorlesungen über dramatische Kunst und Literatur (Lectures on dramatic art and literature)* to denote 'den eigentümlichen Geist der modernen Kunst, im Gegensatz mit der antiken oder klassischen' ('the particular spirit of modern art, in contrast to ancient or classical art') (Heidelberg: Mohr & Winter, 1817, p. 13). Friedrich, in his characteristically unsystematic manner, switched from meaning to meaning according to the needs of the moment. In his *Gespräch über die Poesie (Conversation about Poetry)*, though subscribing in broad outline to the antithesis between the ancient and the romantic, he promptly qualifies it by adding: 'indessen bitte ich Sie doch, nur nicht sogleich anzunehmen, dass mir das Romantische und das Moderne völlig gleich gelte' ('I beg of you, however, not to jump to the conclusion that the romantic and the modern are entirely synonymous to me') (*Kritische Schriften*, ed. W. Rasch, Munich: Hanser Verlag, 1956, p. 324). For him, at this point at least, the romantic is 'nicht sowohl eine Gattung als ein Element der Poesie' ('not only a type but also an element of poetry') (*Kritische*

Schriften, p. 324), and in this sense all creative writing is to some extent romantic. Hence the epithet came to be applied to Shakespeare as well as to Dante and Cervantes. His nearest approach to real definition is in the often quoted phrase: (es) 'ist eben das romantisch, was uns einen sentimentalen Stoff in einer phantastischen Form darstellt' ('that is romantic which depicts emotional matter in an imaginative form') (*Kritische Schriften*, p. 322). However, in the *Geschichte der alten und neuen Literatur (History of ancient and modern literature)*, written some twelve years later, after his conversion to Catholicism, Friedrich Schlegel has abandoned this criterion for he now equates 'romantic' and 'Christian' in such comments as 'Calderon ist . . . unter allen anderen dramatischen Dichtern . . . der christlichste, und eben darum auch der am meisten romantische' ('among all other dramatists, Calderon is the most Christian, and for that reason also the most romantic') (*Geschichte der alten und neuen Literatur*, Munich: Schöningh, 1961, p. 284). Considering the inauspicious debut of the term in literary criticism under the aegis of Friedrich Schlegel, it is hardly surprising that we should encounter difficulties of definition.

In France too the word was given any number of different meanings during the great aesthetic debates of the early nineteenth century. For Mme de Staël 'romantic' was virtually synonymous with Northern, medieval and Christian, as opposed to the Southern, classical and pagan. But for Hugo and Stendhal, as for the majority of their generation, the primary antithesis was between 'romantic' and 'classical', though even in this context it was liable to variations of interpretation. To the rebellious author of *Cromwell* and *Hernani* it was tantamount to the free, the picturesque, the characteristic, which included also the grotesque. To Stendhal it signified quite simply 'modern' or 'contemporary' when he declared in *Racine et Shakespeare* (Paris: Le Divan, 1928, p. 106): 'Tous les grands écrivains ont été romantiques de leur temps'

('All the great writers were romantic in their day'), a contention which he illustrates by reference to the Roman artists who were, according to him, romantic because they portrayed what was true in their day and, therefore, appealing to their public. From this curious standpoint Stendhal deduced his definition of Romanticism:

> Le Romantisme est l'art de présenter aux peuples les oeuvres littéraires qui, dans l'état actuel de leurs habitudes et de leurs croyances, sont susceptibles de leur donner le plus de plaisir possible. Le classicisme, au contraire, leur présente la littérature qui donnait le plus grand plaisir possible à leurs arrière-grandspères.
> (Romanticism is the art of offering people the literary works likely to give them the greatest possible pleasure, having due regard to the habits and beliefs of the time. Classicism, on the other hand, offers them the literature that gave the greatest possible pleasure to their great-grandparents.)
> (*Racine et Shakespeare*, p. 43)

Bizarre though this formulation may seem, it was in fact only one of many then current in France, as is shown by a glance at P. Trahard's *Le Romantisme défini par 'Le Globe'* and the equally useful anthology of *Idées et doctrines littéraires du XIXième siècle* compiled by F. Vial and L. Denise. Romanticism was considered to be protestantism in literature and the arts, or liberalism, or simply poetry as against prose, or the expression of a sensitive heart, or a predilection for the grotesque and fantastic, and so forth.

The most telling comment on this verbal and conceptual confusion is in Musset's satirical *Lettres de Dupuis et Cotonet*. These two worthy citizens of La-Ferté-sous-Jouarre, diligent readers of all the fashionable journals in their pursuit of culture, become increasingly worried as they endeavour to grapple with this word 'romantic', suddenly a favourite of the

Parisian intelligentsia, although in the humbler provinces it had hitherto had 'une signification facile à retenir, il est synonyme d'absurde,' ('a meaning easy to grasp, it is synonymous with absurd') (Paris: Charpentier, 1887, p. 193). At first, they note, the discussion had centred on the grotesque, the picturesque, the description of landscapes in poetry, the revival of the Middle Ages, the use of history. Then, for two years, Dupuis and Cotonet happily cherished the illusion that Romanticism applied only to the theatre to distinguish classical drama from drama that did not observe the unities. They learned that 'le romantisme n'était autre chose que l'alliance du fou et du sérieux, du grotesque et du terrible, du bouffon et de l'horrible, autrement dit, si vous l'aimez mieux, de la comédie et de la tragédie' (p. 194) ('romanticism was nothing other than the combination of the silly and the serious, the grotesque and the terrible, the farcical and the horrible, or, in other words, comedy and tragedy'). But they found the same mingling of the serious and the comic in Aristophanes, and likewise that distinctive melancholy, said to be characteristically Romantic, in Sappho, Plato and Priam. They therefore wondered whether 'le classique ne serait-il donc que l'imitation de la poésie grecque et le romantique que l'imitation des poésies allemandes, anglaises et espagnoles?' (p. 202) ('the classical was then only the imitation of Greek poetry and the romantic the imitation of German, English and Spanish poetry?'); or again: 'ne serait-ce pas, pensâmes-nous, seulement affaire de forme? Ce romantisme indéchiffrable ne consisterait-il pas dans ce vers brisé dont on fait assez de bruit dans le monde?' (p. 203) ('could it, we thought, be merely a matter of form? could this incomprehensible romanticism refer to the break in the verse-line, about which there is so much fuss?'). From 1830 to 1831 they decided it was 'le genre historique'; in 1831 they identified it as 'le genre intime'; from 1832 to 1833 it occurred to them that it might be a philosophical and political system. Finally, however, they came to a fitting conclusion: 'pour en finir, nous croyons que le romantisme consiste à employer tous ces adjectifs et non en autre chose' (p. 220) ('in the last resort, we believe that romanticism is made up of all these adjectives used together, and of nothing else').

England alone was spared these arguments, for the time being at any rate, because the English simply avoided the word and so gracefully side-stepped the issue of its meaning. Wordsworth does not use it in the Preface to the *Lyrical Ballads*; although he is expounding a new type of poetry, he does not call it 'romantic'. Nor is the term to be found in either Shelley's *Defence of Poetry* or Coleridge's *Biographia Literaria*; and when Keats uses it in a letter of 28 June 1818 to his brother George, it is in a non-literary sense as he mentions seeing 'the names of romantic misses on the inn window panes.' The term was not in fact applied to the English literature of the early nineteenth century until much later, so that Carlyle could write in 1831, in an article on Schiller: 'we are troubled with no controversies on Romanticism and Classicism' (Carlyle, *Miscellanies*, London, 1890, vol. iii, p. 71). There was certainly talk of the Lake School, the Satanic School, etc., but not of the Romantic School. This reticence in introducing the term into the literary context is all the more surprising in view of the word's English origins.

The origins of 'romantic'

Since the Romantics themselves were so equivocal in their usage, it is worth asking at this point in our search for clarity whence they derived the word and what had been its primary significance. An invaluable inquiry into this subject was carried out by Logan Pearsall Smith, whose essay 'Four Romantic Words' is indispensable to any student of this period. The synoptic tables compiled by F. Baldensperger along with his article 'Pour une interprétation équitable du romantisme européen' are also illuminating while the recent weighty volume '*Romantic*' *and Its Cognates: The European History of a Word* (ed. H. Eichner) will certainly become the definitive work for scholarly purposes.

In the early Middle Ages, 'romance' denoted the new vernacular languages in distinction to the learned tongue, Latin. So 'enromancier' and 'romançar' meant to translate or compose books in the vernacular. Such a book was called a 'romanz', 'roman' or 'romance'; in Old French, for instance, 'roman' described a courtly romance in verse as well as a popular story. The characteristics of these tales of love, adventure and the vagaries of the imagination soon came to be associated with the word itself.

But it was in England that the term first became familiar and widely diffused; indeed it has been called one of the most notable English contributions to European thought. At first it was connected with the old romances, tales of chivalry, characterized by high-flown sentiments, improbability, exaggeration, unreality – in short, elements diametrically opposed to a sober, rational view of life. So 'romantic' was used in such phrases as 'wild romantic tales' to denote 'false', 'fictitious', 'imaginary'. During the Age of Reason in the seventeenth century, in a world ruled by order and absolute truth, the word inevitably fell into increasing disrepute so that it is found alongside 'chimerical', 'bombastic', 'ridiculous', 'childish'. 'Romantic absurdities and incredible fictions' is a typical usage in a climate that prized correctness above imagination.

Not until the gradual, still only half-conscious shift of feeling in England in the early eighteenth century did the word begin to recover status, to acquire fresh meanings. From serving merely as a term of depreciation, it came to express approval now: as early as 1711 'romantic' occurs in association with 'fine'. At roughly the same time the old romances were rehabilitated with the nascent interest in the Middle Ages, the Elizabethan period, the Gothic and Spenser. 'Romantic' could then mean 'captivating to the imagination', a faculty no longer so distrusted as lawless. Moreover, it was applied to landscapes and scenes in nature too, again in a positive sense, often to describe the mountains, forests, and wild places commonly the setting for the old romances. Thus by about the mid-eighteenth century it carries already a dual meaning: the original one, i.e. redolent or suggestive of the old romances, and an elaboration that adumbrated its appeal to the imagination and feelings.

This was the time when it was imported into France. Attempts were made to render it by its native equivalents, 'romanesque' or 'pittoresque' before 'romantique' was accepted as an English loan word. As a 'mot Anglais' ('English word') it was used by Letourneur, the translator of Shakespeare and Ossian, and also by the Marquis de Girardin in a book on landscape gardening. While 'pittoresque' specified a visual attraction, 'romantique' referred above all to the emotional response evoked by a scene. It is with this connotation that it features in the famous sentence at the opening of the second paragraph of the fifth 'promenade' of Rousseau's *Rêveries du Promeneur Solitaire (Musings of the Solitary Stroller)*: 'Les rives du lac de Bienne sont plus sauvages et romantiques que celles du lac de Genève' ('the shores of lake Bienne are more wild and romantic than those of lake Geneva'). This was indeed still its main meaning in 1798 according to the entry in the Dictionary of the French Acadamy: 'Il se dit ordinairement des lieux, des paysages qui rappellent à l'imagination les descriptions des poèmes et des romans' ('It is usually said of places and landscapes which recall to the imagination descriptions in poems and novels'). Its fate was very similar in Germany where it arrived from England with Thomson's *Seasons*. As in France, the neologism 'romantisch', formed on the English analogy, supplanted the older word 'romanhaft' and was applied to wild landscapes.

'Romantic' was not, therefore, from its inception a term of

artistic criticism; it denoted fundamentally a turn of mind that looked favourably on things of an imaginative and emotional kind. Its transference to the literary sphere is a relatively late usage, thought to date from Friedrich Schlegel's 125-page cogitations of 1797. It is important to know this sequence, to realize that the word was already loaded with meaning when it was grafted on to the arts. The vital changes that led up to the emergence of the Romantic movement in literature occurred not with the appearance of the word as a term of literary criticism, but with the deep-seated modification of attitudes that evolved in the course of the eighteenth century. For the term 'romantic' and the associated words 'originality', 'creation' and 'genius' could only come to the fore as a result of the basic re-orientation of human values that affected not only styles of writing but the total view of man and nature. The Romantic movement is the culmination of that long process of change, and if we wish to grasp its essential meaning, we must look to its evolution rather than to a slick catch-word of definition.

2
The pre-history of the Romantic movement

The roots of the Romantic movement lie in the eighteenth century in a series of interlocking trends of cumulative effect: the decline of the Neo-classical system led to the questionings of the Enlightenment, which in turn was conducive to the infiltration of the new notions current in the latter half of the century. Although the appellation 'pre-Romantic' is generally reserved for certain writers and thinkers who were direct fore-runners of the Romantics in ideas or style (e.g. Rousseau, Young, Macpherson, Bernardin de Saint-Pierre), in a wider sense the term is appropriate to the entire line of development in the eighteenth century, in so far as it paved the way for the crystallization of the Romantic movement. A major re-orientation of critical standards and methods was an essential pre-condition for the blossoming of Romanticism, and this took place in the course of the eighteenth century. Thus the Romantic movement, though it effected a literary revolution at its decisive break-through, was in itself in fact the product of a protracted process of evolution. The direction and form of this evolution points to the nature of the Romantic revolution.

The decline of the Neo-classical system

The period that equated 'romantic' with 'chimerical' and 'ridiculous' was that of Neo-classicism, which was at its height in the seventeenth century, notably in France. Since the revival of Classical standards in the Renaissance, the main concern had been the establishment, elaboration and spread of a view of literature inherited from Greek and Roman antiquity. The chief sources of aesthetic ideas were, for over two centuries, Aristotle, Horace, Quintilian and Longinus. The major topic of discussion was the revival and imitation of the Ancients, who enjoyed unlimited authority and inspired a strong craving to conform to their patterns. This is most evident in France, where the Neo-classical attitude was codified by critics as powerful as Boileau and where the strict observance of the three unities was considered of paramount importance. Moreover, the passage of time brought an increasing emphasis on a merely repetitive formalism, a hollow clinging to the outer practices of Neo-classicism without any deeper understanding of its aims such as had inspired the great poets of the seventeenth century. This dogmatism was buttressed in France by the dominance of an absolute monarchy allied to the Catholic Church so that the literary as well as the political and religious regime was close to totalitarianism. In the England of parliamentary rule and easy-going Protestantism there was never the same degree of conformity; the approach to both political organization and literary taste was far more flexible, not to say unsystematic, partly no doubt as a result of Shakespeare's disregard of the Neo-classical canons. It is, nevertheless, worth recalling that the early eighteenth century could and did dismiss *Hamlet* on the grounds of its 'incorrectness'.

The authoritarianism of the Neo-classical period stemmed from an unqualified belief in the powers of the mind, the intellect, in short, reason. Descartes in his famous 'Cogito ergo sum' deduced the very existence of man from his powers of thought; in Germany the philosopher Christian Wolff conceived God as 'reiner Verstand' ('pure reason') and the world as a mechanism that functioned logically according to set laws, while in England Pope maintained, in the *Essay on Man* 'that REASON alone countervails all the other faculties'.

The scientific discoveries of the age, specially those of Newton, helped to foster the conviction that all things were knowable, and what is more, knowable by means of rational understanding. This total commitment to, indeed trust in, reason was what Isaiah Berlin had very aptly called the backbone of European thought for generations – the backbone which the Romantics were to crack.

In the arts, as in politics, ethics and morals, the Neoclassicists hoped to do what Newton had achieved in physics: to discern universal truths and establish standards of lasting validity. Hence they sought to formulate once and for all the basic 'laws' of aesthetics, the rules of writing which, properly observed, would guarantee a correct (and therefore necessarily good) composition, just as a recipe, carefully followed, will produce a fine dish. The artist, like the scientist, was expected to operate by calculation, judgement and reason, for, to borrow La Bruyère's revealing comparison, the making of a book was considered a task like the making of a clock. Art was thus conceived as a reasonable and reasoned imitation of reality, the artist as a skilful manipulator, and the ultimate aim of the whole exercise as an intellectual statement of moral precepts, in which pleasure was no more than a means to an end. This view is well illustrated by Gottsched's instructions for 'the making of a good tragedy' from his *Kritische Dichtkunst (Ars Poetica)* of 1730:

Der Poet wählet sich einen moralischen Lehrsatz, den er seinen Zuschauern auf eine sinnliche Art einprägen will. Dazu ersinnt er sich eine allgemeine Fabel, daraus die Wahrheit seines Satzes erhellet. Hiernächst sucht er in der Historie solche berühmte Leute, denen etwas Ähnliches begegnet ist, und von diesen entlehnet er die Namen vor die Personen seiner Fabel, um derselben also ein Ansehen zu geben. Er erdenket sodann alle Umstände dazu, um die Hauptfabel recht wahrscheinlich zu machen, und das werden die Zwischenfabeln oder Episodia genannt. Dieses teilt er denn in fünf Stücke ein, die ungefähr gleich gross sind, und ordnet sie so, dass natürlicherweise das letztere aus dem vorhergehenden fliesset, bekümmert sich aber weiter nicht, ob alles in der Historie so vorgegangen oder ob alle Nebenpersonen wirklich so und nicht anders geheissen.

(Let the poet first choose a moral precept which he wants to impress on his audience by means of the senses. Then he invents a general story to illustrate the truth of his precept. Next he looks in history for famous people to whom something similar has happened, and from them he borrows names for the characters in his story in order to give it a semblance of reality. After this he thinks up all the attendant circumstances necessary to make the main story really probable, and these are called the sub-plots or episodes. He then divides his material into five pieces, all of approximately equal length, and arranges them so that each section follows from the preceding one, but he does not bother further whether everything corresponds to the historical happenings, nor whether the subsidiary characters bore these or other names.)

That this conception of art and of the artist's role was in the long run untenable is self-evident, whatever arguments may be advanced in its defence. The weaknesses of Neo-classical aesthetics are only too numerous: its view of art was extreme in its weighting towards the rational, simplified to the point of standardization and so rigid as to induce sterility, or at least a repetition of a fixed pattern. It had also many contradictions concealed in its system, as Wellek has pointed out in his lucid and fair assessment of the Neo-classical position in the first chapter of his *History of Modern Criticism* (Vol. i, pp. 12–30), and as these contradictions were opened up, there was a growing unease with the doctrine as a whole. Its fabric began to dissolve as men became increasingly conscious of the vast areas which it had chosen to ignore completely. This in fact was its most damning defect, that it took virtually no account of the *irrational* aspects of the creative process: what we call rather vaguely 'inspiration', the inner impetus of the artist, and the instinctive response on the part of the reader. In keeping with this omission, the imagination was relegated to a very minor role because it was considered a mere caprice, incapable of producing a judicious poem. Its function was almost exclusively decorative: the addition of 'wit' to truths already known. Thus Gray, when asked by an aspiring poet how to turn a flat piece of prose into a poem, advised him to 'twirl it a little into an apophthegm, stick a flower in it, gild it with a costly expression' (T. Gray, *Correspondence with William Mason*, London, 1853, p. 146). Far from being the mainspring of poetry, the imagination was no more than a storehouse of images in some remote attic of the brain. The imitative, rationalistic view of art offered no real scope for the individual imagination: this was the cardinal source of its inadequacy and the eventual cause of its decline in the eighteenth century.

The dissolution of the Neo-classical system meant more than the replacement of one set of aesthetics by another. Neo-classicism had not only been the dominant attitude for a considerable period, and had enjoyed a veneration reflected from its Classical antecedents. It had also offered men a coherent, stable view of the world, derived from the certainty of a well-established order in the universe, thereby giving to literature too a sure frame of reference. With the abandonment of the old system, its sense of security was lost in life as in art. This is a break of such far-reaching consequences that its effects, even today, can hardly be overestimated. Our relativism, our ambivalence, our hesitations of judgement, our unwillingness (or inability?) to settle on any firm standards – all these are, in the last resort, developments from that crucial jettisoning of the Neo-classical definities and the tentative questionings of the Enlightenment. The objective order was slowly and surely displaced by a principle of subjective reference.

The questionings of the Enlightenment

The dawn of the Enlightenment was like the opening of shutters that had been tightly clamped down. The image of increasing light is very appropriately suggested in its name in the three major European languages: Enlightenment, *Lumières* and *Aufklärung*, of which the latter two also imply the idea of light and clarity ('*lumière*' and '*klar*'). This is apposite in that the essence of the Enlightenment is a quest for new light on issues that had become stereotyped. What had hitherto been accepted (for instance, the absolute validity of the three unities in drama) was now questioned as the basic Neo-classical assumptions were re-examined in an attempt to separate the chaff from the grain. This process of critical assessment was a slow one, and it was still founded on a respect for reason. There was neither blatant defiance of the Neo-classical canons nor a wholesale introduction of startlingly new ideas; the shift of emphasis was reasoned and reasoning and the mood was one of cautious compromise. The change of tone is, however, unmistakable: from the old dogmatism to a far greater flexibility that was ready to admit into aesthetic discussion certain notions (e.g. genius, beauty, phantasy) beyond the domain of reason. During the Enlightenment these factors came to be recognized as an integral part of the work of art.

The pace and extent of the advance during the Enlightenment was directly related to the strength of the Neo-classical conventions. Thus it was slowest in France, the land of Descartes, where the long-established traditions were so deeply entrenched as to persist far into the eighteenth century. As late as 1799 La Harpe, in his *Cours de littérature ancienne et moderne* still presented a codified summary of the old outlook with its charactersitic insistence on the eternal principles, the rules of literature. Voltaire too, in spite of his political radicalism, was a conservative in literary matters, looking back with a nostalgic admiration to the age of Racine. Though opposed to excessive rationalism and summary judgements according to immutable criteria, Voltaire did stress the need for good taste, moderation, decorum, what was called *bienséance* in art. His concessions are grudging: in admitting 'enthusiasm' into his *Dictionnaire philosophique*, he demands that it must always be 'reasonable', i.e. held in check by an intellectual control. When he wrote to a friend in 1753: 'Je n'estime la poésie qu'autant qu'elle est l'ornement de la raison' ('I value poetry only in so far as it is an ornament of reason') (F. Vial and L. Denise, *Idées et doctrines littéraires du XVIIIième siècle*, p. 164), he revealed the order of priorities in his mind, and there can be no doubt that reason headed the list. It was by no means as simple for Diderot, who put forward many progressive ideas in the prefaces to *Le Fils naturel* (1757) and *Le Père de famille* (1758). In place of the lofty type of tragedy hitherto customary and upheld by Voltaire, Diderot here advocated 'domestic' tragedy, in which realistic devices could be used to intensify the emotional effect. Moreover, Diderot extolled the power of genius over the authority of the rules, useful though these could be in an age of decadence. On the whole he considered rationalization to be detrimental to poetry, and in *Le Rêve de d'Alembert (The Dream of d'Alembert*, 1769) he seems to be hinting at a theory of imagination as a perception of hidden analogies. Had he developed or even only sustained these notions, Diderot would have been in the forefront of the Enlightenment. Indeed *Le Neveu de Rameau* (1762) presents the Enlightenment's own profoundest self-criticism in its confrontation between the eighteenth century's right-minded conformist sage and the free-flowing demonic inventiveness of the social parasite, the marginal man, who foreshadows both the Romantic hero and the modern anti-hero. As he grew older, however, partly under the government's threats to radical writers, Diderot became increasingly circumspect and prudent. His final position is baffling: he appears unable to choose between two worlds, fascinated by Shakespeare, yet faithful to the native creed. Diderot's ambiguous attitude is in many ways symptomatic of eighteenth-century France, of a period of transition that no longer wholeheartedly espoused the ideals of the previous century without, however, going so far as to abandon them. It is no coincidence that the term *Lumières* has relatively little currency in France. The timidity of its Enlightenment, its comparative backwardness in emancipating itself from the Neo-classical system were to prove important factors in shaping the character of the French Romantic movement.

The Enlightenment was a time of complex countercurrents in English literature too. While it is tempting to emphasize the many departures from outworn theories and practices, it is well to remember that this was also the age of Johnson. His massive personality looms large, and if not reactionary, he was stoutly conservative in his basically rationalistic views, representing a position not unlike that of Voltaire in France. Reason in fact continued to enjoy considerable prestige, specially in the attenuated guise of reasonableness, which was tantamount to sound common sense. Herein lies perhaps a typically English example of compromise: whereas in France the rules were arbitrarily imposed as a *conditio sine qua non* of art, in England they were considered the outcome of good sense and sound reason rather than absolute authority. Consequently they became for the French a tyrannical yoke, which could only be cast off eventually by outright rebellion, while in England they were continuously tempered and modified to fit changing conceptions of what was reasonable practice. Even Pope conceded in his *Essay on Criticism* (1711) that

> Those RULES of old discovered, not devis'd,
> Are nature still, but nature methodiz'd.

Dryden went much further when he advocated that rules should be stretched or broken in preference to sacrificing any great beauty. This is a most important opinion because it shows the emergence of a new approach in literary criticism: the evaluation of a work of art by positive aesthetic standards, i.e. the appreciation of its beauties, rather than by the negative, pedantic yardstick of counting its infringements of the rules. This new attitude, in turn, discouraged too strict a formalism, and there were numerous protests against making poetry 'a mere mechanical art' as well as against over-much moralizing didacticism. The Neo-classical tenets were thus questioned sooner and more radically in England than in France, and they were more readily refashioned because they had never achieved the same intransigent power as in the France of the seventeenth century. The English could and did look back to their pre-Restoration heritage, to Shakespeare and the Elizabethans, who provided models quite different from the Classical tradition. There was, therefore, a far greater freedom, range and variety in Augustan writing than in the comparable period in France. Elegance, moderation and correctness were indeed highly prized; but at the same time there is also evidence of a certain agility in both thought and expression that is the very epitome of the Enlightenment. The England of the mid-eighteenth century was clearly open to new ideas.

This is even more true of Germany, partly because it had at this point nothing in its history comparable to Shakespeare and the Elizabethans in England or the French 'golden age' of Corneille, Racine, Molière, etc. At the start of the Enlightenment Germany was very much the poor relation in Europe, a fragmentary patchwork of small states without a unifying cultural centre, economically backward, impoverished, still suffering from the backwash of the Thirty Years' War. In many respects the state of affairs in Germany in the first half of the eighteenth century is the antithesis to that in France: on one side of the Rhine a proud awareness of a brilliant past, leading naturally to a reluctance to depart from the practices that had produced so glorious a harvest; whereas on the opposite bank, little sense of achievement in the past, and consequently a far greater willingness to experiment with new ideas and techniques. For in the long run it was, paradoxically, the initial backwardness of Germany that was to make her the leader of the Romantic movement in Europe, where France, with her powerful Classical tradition, lagged behind. The failure of Gottsched's attempt to introduce the Neo-classical system into Germany proved fortunate; firstly because it meant that there was no burden of accepted practice to hinder progress, and secondly because Gottsched's extreme views provoked the opposition of Bodmer and Breitinger. Not that these two Swiss critics were particularly revolutionary in their ideas; their *Kritische Dichtkunst (Ars Poetica)* of 1739 is still redolent of Neo-classical attitudes, but there is a distinct advance in the recognition that poetry springs not from the intellect but from the spirit and the imagination. Bodmer even had some inkling of the creative powers of the imagination, which he called more potent than 'alle Zauberer der Welt' (all the magicians in the world') (W. Burkhard (ed.), *Schriftwerke deutscher Sprache*, Aarau: Sauerländer, 1953, vol. 2, p. 31). By an interesting coincidence that phrase dates from the same year, 1741, when Hume maintained in his essay *Of the Standard of Taste* that 'to check the sallies of the imagination, and to reduce every expression to geometrical truth and exactness, would be the most contrary to the laws of criticism.' The questioning note of critical reassessment is as plain in Hume as in Bodmer and Breitinger.

Nowhere is this more evident than in the criticism of

Lessing, who appears the very incarantion of the Enlightenment. Drawing on his profound knowledge of the Classics, Lessing was able to analyse their actual practices and to compare them with modern usage. The best example of this method is in section XLVI of the *Hamburgische Dramaturgie*, where he demonstrates the sensible, even profitable application of the unities in Classical drama as against the dogmatic adherence of the French to rules that became senseless with the abolition of the Chorus. The Neo-classical tenets are here not merely questioned, but made to seem absurd and hypocritical. And Lessing's criticism is so convincing because he is eminently reasonable in the logical sequence of his thought and the close-knit structure of his style. These are not the wild shots of an angry opponent, but the devastatingly thorough attack of the moderate man, very sure in his aim. Nor was Lessing just a destructive critic; each of his onslaughts has its complement of constructive suggestions. For instance, the section on the observance of the unities points to the significance of the 'irregular' English drama, adding the comment: 'Möchten meinetwegen Voltaires und Maffeis *Mérope* acht Tage dauern und an sieben Orten in Griechenland spielen! Möchten sie aber nur die Schönheiten haben, die mich diese Pedantereien vergessen machen' ('For all I care, Voltaire's and Maffei's *Mérope* could go on for eight days and be set in seven different places in Greece! But would that they were of a beauty to make me forget these pedantic considerations') (W. Burkhard, *op. cit.*, vol. ii, p. 98). This implies the same vital change in critical standards as Dryden's identical preference of great beauty over the rules.

With its questionings the Enlightenment achieved emancipation from the authoritarianism of the Neo-classical creed. The advances were perhaps still only modest, but the trend is clear enough: away from the neat, finite, regular schemes of the old system towards a growing appreciation of the irregular beauties of the irrational imagination.

The innovations of Pre-Romanticism

While the old was disintegrating under the questionings of the Enlightenment, the new was already appearing in the works of those writers of the mid- and later eighteenth century now known as 'Pre-Romantics'. This is an awkward portmanteau term, used as vaguely as 'romantic' itself, and, of course, meaningful only in relation to the major movement which it pre-figured in various ways. As a critical term it is useful to denote the many innovations in attitudes, ideas and techniques introduced at this time as part of the tentative search for something to replace the Neo-classical system of aesthetics and style of writing. In its positive beginnings Pre-Romanticism is complementary to the Enlightenment which was primarily directed towards a critical assessment of past, received notions. At some points the two trends interlock, as in the enthusiasm for Shakespeare and in the growing importance attached to the imagination of the genius. But whereas the Enlightenment represents a critique of the old, Pre-Romanticism is inspired by a real revulsion from all that Neo-classicism was thought to stand for: dull rules, superficial elegance, formality, orderliness, finite views, artificiality, convention, didacticism, courtly civilization, the preservation of the *status quo*. Not that the Pre-Romantics had any coherent programme to replace the old system – that in itself would have savoured too much of a rational approach. Hence the essentially haphazard, sporadic character of Pre-Romanticism which is made up of a number of individual starts rather than a concerted effort. Nevertheless certain common factors can be discerned in disparate works of the years 1740–80 which reveal the dominant concerns of this period. In every field the emphasis was on the natural in contrast to the rational, the spontaneous in place of the calculated, freedom instead of regimentation. This freedom led to the bewildering variety in the manifestations of Pre-Romanticism, but the basic trend is everywhere evident: in the new modes of feeling and their more direct expression, in the choice of new pastures and also in the new aesthetics.

New modes of feeling

Just as the Neo-classical period earned its alternative name, the Age of Reason, so Pre-Romanticism is rightly regarded as the Age of Sensibility. As early as 1739 Hume had maintained in the *Treatise of Human Nature* (Book II, part iii, section 3) that 'reason is, and ought only to be the slave of the passions.' If not the passions in our sense of the word, at least sensibility came to supersede reason as the touchstone to life when the emotional susceptibility of a tender heart was valued more highly than the sound judgement of a cool head. The great popularity of the plays of Cibber and Steele with their touching scenes and declamatory speeches is indicative of the change of taste and of attitude. This had its parallel in France in the so-called *comédies larmoyantes* (tearful comedies) of La Chaussée, and in Germany in the soulful poetry of Klopstock. It was, however, in the novel, and particularly in the English novel, that sensibility found its main expression in the mid-eighteenth century, perhaps because the new could most easily triumph where the old was least firmly established, i.e. in England and in prose. Prévost's *Manon Lescaut* (1735), Rousseau's *La Nouvelle Héloïse* (1761) and Goethe's *Die Leiden des jungen Werthers* (*The Sufferings of young Werther*, 1774) are the only major Continental examples to place beside a whole galaxy of English novels: Richardson's *Pamela* (1740), *Clarissa Harlowe* (1747), *Sir Charles Grandison* (1754), Goldsmith's *Vicar of Wakefield* (1766), Sterne's *Sentimental Journey* (1768), Henry Mackenzie's *Man of Feeling* (1771) and Henry Brooke's *Juliet Grenville; or the History of the Human Heart* (1774). This last subtitle is appropriate to almost all these novels, which tell, in an effusive manner, of the misfortunes and problems of the virtuous and which seek to move and instruct by arousing pity for the innocent victims. The plots and situations are less of importance in themselves in these long, often repetitive tales than as an occasion for the unbridled display of sentiment. The following passage from *Clarissa Harlowe* well conveys the flavour of these novels:

> It seems, when she read the billet – Now indeed, said she, am I a lost creature! O the poor Clarissa Harlowe!
>
> She tore off her head-clothes; inquiring where I was: and in she came, her shining tresses flowing about her neck; her ruffles torn, and hanging in tatters about her snowy hands; with her arms spread out; her eyes wildly turned, as if starting from their orbits. Down sunk she at my feet, as soon as she approached me; her charming bosom heaving to her uplifted face; and clasping her arms about my knees, Dear Lovelace, said she, if ever – if ever – if ever – and, unable to speak another word, quitting her clasping hold, down prostrate on the floor sunk she, neither in a fit nor out of one.
>
> . . . .
>
> I lifted her, however, into a chair; and in words of disordered passion, told her, all her fears were needless: wondered at them; begged of her to be pacified; brought her reliance on my faith and honour: and revowed all my old vows, and poured forth new ones.
>
> At last, with a heart-breaking sob, I see, I see, Mr Lovelace, in broken sentences she spoke, I see, I see – that at last – I am ruined! Ruined, if *your* pity – let me implore your pity! And down on her bosom, like a half-broken-stalked lily, top-heavy with the overcharging dews of the morning, sunk her head, with a sigh that went to my heart.
>
> (London: Dent, 1962, vol. iii, pp. 192–3)

Extravagant though such an effusion may seem to us, it had an immense attraction to its age throughout Europe as a welcome change from the aridity of much early eighteenth-century writing. Widely translated and imitated, Richardson's novels were admired by Rousseau, Diderot, Goethe and Herder in a panegyric of praise. Besides his free expression of sentiment, Richardson was also important for the prominence he gave to the letter-form which fostered a subjective approach through the author's identification with his persona so that the situation and sentiment are presented from within. In both these respects Richardson pointed forward to Romanticism.

So did the vogue for the 'Gothic' in architecture and in literature in the second half of the eighteenth century (see 'The Gothic Background' in Peter Quennell's *Romantic England: Writing and Painting 1717–1851*). Its appeal too was addressed to the sensibility, although the response it evoked was a shudder of fear, a vicarious thrill as the reader is lured into the realm of the supernatural and the horrid. Walpole's *Castle of Otranto* (1764), Beckford's *Vathek* (1786), Mrs Radcliffe's *Mysteries of Udolpho* (1794) and Lewis's *The Monk* (1796) were not only avidly read at the time but also mark the beginning of one strand of Romanticism. This fascination with the demonic was to continue throughout the nineteenth century in such works are Mary Shelley's *Frankenstein* (1832), many of the tales of E. T. A. Hoffman and of Edgar Allan Poe, not to mention the writings of the so-called Decadents. Strange though it seems beside the traditional Romantic cult of beauty, this penchant towards the darkly mysterious aspects of life represents another facet of the Romantic interest in the exceptional and also the urge to explore the uncharted (see M. Praz, *The Romantic Agony*).

When the sensitive heart turned inwards to contemplate itself it became increasingly conscious of its own melancholy. This tendency was fostered by the religious movements of the day, such as Methodism in England and Pietism in Germany, both of which exalted religious sentiments in fervid devotional hymns and stressed the role of the individual soul and of

intimate revelation. Although Methodism had also a more
practical side in its social work, it did, like Pietism, make men
aware of the fleetingness and vanity of human life, the sadness
of human destiny. This theme was soon evident in poetry in
such works as Gray's *Elegy written in a Country Churchyard*
(1742–51), Young's *Night Thoughts* (1742) and Hervey's
Meditations among the Tombs (1748). Their titles alone
explain why these poems have been grouped together as 'la
poésie de la nuit et des tombeaux' ('the poetry of night and
tombs') (see P. van Tieghem, *La poésie de la nuit et des tombeaux*). In all these laments on the fate of man, the sentimental
strain is dominant in place of the rather crude, macabre realism
common in the medieval dance of the skeletons. Now the
physical recedes before the emotional as images of decay
(graveyards, ruins, ancient cloisters) provoke mournful reflections. Gray's *Elegy* has many of the elements, both
thematic and technical, of this melancholy poetry: the churchyard, the tombs pointing to the transience of life, the twilight
of the close of the day, solitude, solemnity, the melodiousness
of the atmospheric description in which all the details are
subdued to the total effect, the stirrings of a poetic imagination
beginning to act through images at once subtle and potent.
Equally important in this context are Young's *Night Thoughts*;
the extraordinary vogue for this long, lugubrious poem is a
telling comment on the taste of the Age of Sensibility. Young
portrays himself as a lonely old man, bereft of wife, daughter
and friend, spending sleepless nights in gloomy reflections.

> Why then their loss deplore that are not lost?
> Why wanders wretched thought their tombs around,
> In infidel distress? Are angels there?
> Slumbers, raked up in dust, ethereal fire?
>   They live! they greatly live a life on earth
> Unkindled, unconceiv'd; and from an eye
> Of tenderness let heavenly pity fall

On me, more justly number'd with the dead.
This is the desert, this the solitude:
How populous, how vital, is the grave!
This is creation's melancholy vault,
The vale funereal, the sad cypress gloom;
The land of apparitions, empty shades!
All, all on earth, is shadow, all beyond
Is substance; the reverse is Folly's creed:
How solid all, where change shall be no more!

(*Night I*, London: Rivington, 1813, p. 7)

This effusion of woeful feelings had the same appeal as the sentimental novel. The flow of emotion, the shadowy, mysterious settings, the grandiose phrases, the innate melancholy: all these clearly foreshadow Romantic writing.

The new modes of feeling as well as the new means of expression are already clearly present in Rousseau's *Rêveries du promeneur solitaire (Musings of a Solitary Stroller*, 1782), a work that is radically subjective in both form and content. In a loosely structured series of 'musings', linked by a fluid association of images and ideas, Rousseau gives voice to his reactions, his sentiments, his moods. The centre of gravity resides in the personality of the 'stroller' that here finds full and spontaneous self-expression. With the *Rêveries* the individual, at the culmination of his gradual rise in stature, attains the position of pre-eminence that was to be characteristic of Romanticism.

New pastures

The Pre-Romantics sought the natural and spontaneous not only in the inner realm of the emotions but also in the outer world. Hence they developed a passionate interest in areas diametrically opposed to the artificiality of urban and, more specifically, courtly life, i.e. in nature and in 'simple' primitive society. The young Marie-Antoinette's flight from the

splendid palace of Versailles to play at shepherds and shep-
herdesses in her mock village, the Petit Trianon, is symbolical
of this trend.

This 'return to nature' implied a totally new conception of
the outer world. The fundamental change can be summarized
in two words: from a mechanistic to an organic view. For
Descartes and his fellow rationalists the world had been a
machine, engineered by God in the beginning and functioning
according to set principles; man, with his intellect, was the king
of this universe, taming that savage object, nature, by ordering
it into symmetrical flower-beds, neat hedges and straight paths
in the manner of the formal French gardens. The fashion in
the mid-eighteenth century for the picturesque English style
of landscape gardening was symptomatic of, and also instru-
mental in the change of attitude. From being a mere tool of
man, nature was first granted an autonomous existence, and
poets, instead of using vague, standard phrases, began actually
to observe and to describe what they had seen. This was the
mainspring of such works as Thomson's *The Seasons* (1730),
Haller's *Die Alpen* (1729) and Saint-Lambert's *Les Saisons*
(1769). Perhaps this observation of nature led to the recognition of its dynamic, organic character with an ever-changing
life of its own, as varied in mood as man himself. From this it
was but a short step to that association of the moods of man
and of nature so common in Romantic poetry. It occurs already
during the Pre-Romantic period when sensibility intervenes
to turn the objective portrayal of nature into a subjective
feeling for nature. The mood of nature is seen more and more
in relation to man's sentiments in, for instance, the opening
lines of Gray's *Elegy*, in some of the poems of Cowper and of
Delille, and most notably in Goethe's early lyric poetry:

> Wie herrlich leuchtet
> Mir die Natur
> (How resplendent nature is for me)

he exclaims at the beginning of *Mailied (May-song* 1771), a lyric that celebrates, in a complete fusion of poet and nature, the indissoluble joys of young love and of spring. Such interpenetration of man and nature is frequent in Romantic poetry and prose (and indeed painting too) when the natural milieu is assimilated to the individual's state of mind. The prototype of this approach, generally known as *paysage état d'âme* (literally: landscape state of mind), is found in Rousseau's *Rêveries:*

Depuis quelques jours on avait achevé la vendange; les promeneurs de la ville s'étaient déjà retirés; les paysans aussi quittaient les champs jusqu'aux travaux d'hiver. La campagne, encore verte et riante, mais défeuillée en partie, et déjà presque déserte, offrait partout l'image de la solitude et des approches de l'hiver. Il résultait de son aspect un mélange d'impression douce et triste, trop analogue à mon âge et à mon sort pour que je ne m'en fisse pas l'application. Je me voyais au déclin d'une vie innocente et infortunée, l'âme encore pleine de sentiments vivaces, et l'esprit encore orné de quelques fleurs, mais déjà flétries par la tristesse et desséchées par les ennuis. Seul et délaissé, je sentais venir le froid des premières glaces . . .

(Paris: Garnier Flammarion, 1964, p. 47)

(Some days earlier the grape-harvest had been finished; the townspeople had given up their excursions into the country; the peasants too were leaving the fields until the time of the winter tasks. The countryside, still green and smiling, but losing some of its leaves and already nearly deserted, suggested an image of solitude and approaching winter. Its appearance evoked a sweet, sad sensation, too like my own time of life and my own fate for me not to perceive its aptness. I saw myself at the wane of an innocent, unfortunate life; my soul was still alive with feeling, my mind still

> embellished with a few flowers already withered by sadness and dried up by worries. Alone and forsaken, I felt the coming cold of the first frosty days . . .)

Such a passage clearly brings us to the threshold of Romanticism.

Rousseau was also decisive in the development of the 'simple life' syndrome and its associated notion of the 'noble savage'. This was not entirely new in literature; *Robinson Crusoe* (1719) is still one of the outstanding examples of the 'desert island' story. But it was Rousseau who grafted on to the tale of adventure an ideology that left its trace in the Romantics' Utopian streak, in Coleridge's and Southey's Pantisocratic project as well as in Blake's vision of a Golden Age. In the *Discours sur l'origine de l'inégalité parmi les hommes* (*Discourse on the origins of inequality among men*, 1755) Rousseau maintained that decadence stems from civilization, particularly from the ownership of property, which resulted in inequality and thence envy and depravity. His suggested remedy was the famous 'return to nature', to what he called 'the first social state', a rudimentary communal organization based on sharing. The appeal of this democratic doctrine to an age under the sway of a powerful land-owning aristocracy is obvious. It led to a widespread idealization of 'innocent' society in the 'natural' state and of 'primitive' man, although these terms were interpreted in a hazy fashion. Men sought out such ideal societies and thought to find them either in remote parts of the world or in the past.

So there was a whole spate of works that devolved from the discovery of the virtues of the 'natural'. There were tales with an exotic milieu, such as Bernardin de Saint-Pierre's *La Chaumière indienne* (*The Indian Hut*, 1790) and *Paul et Virginie* (1788), an island idyll that extols the moral beauty of the natural state and shows how tragedy comes from contact with the avarice of European civilization; or Chateaubriand's

Atala (1801) and *René* (1805), set among the Natchez, a noble, primitive American tribe. There were works concerned with the actions of natural man and the idea of natural justice: for instance Goethe's *Götz von Berlichingen* (1773) and Schiller's *Die Räuber (The Robbers,* 1781). There was lively interest also in the spontaneous utterances of natural man in the folk-songs and tales of the past published in such collections as Percy's *Reliques* (1765) and Herder's *Stimmen der Völker (Voices of the People,* 1778). This moreover, is the context of the Celtic revival and of Macpherson's *Poems of Ossian* (1762) which literally took Europe by storm in a frenzy of translations, imitations, further elaborations in poetry, drama, opera, painting and even clothing (see P. van Tieghem, *Ossian et l'ossianisme dans la littérature européenne au XVIIIième siècle).* Macpherson presented this cycle of prose poems, in an accompanying learned dissertation, as versions of an ancient Gaelic bard, the last scion of an extinct race, singing of their heroic and sentimental exploits. The fact that Ossian was placed beside Shakespeare (even by the young Goethe) shows how seriously these poems were taken. Their attraction was manifold: as the 'natural' poetry of primitive man and as a picture of a primitive society, as an expression of melancholy sensibility, as an evocation of the picturesque Northern landscape shrouded in dark mists, as a revelation of pagan Celtic (i.e. anti-Classical) mythology (the names alone were evocative: Cuthullin, Dar-thulla, Cathmor, Temora, Cuthona, Conlath, Fingal, etc.), as a dramatic recital of stirring intrigues reminiscent of the old romances, and last, but by no means least, as a new poetic style, rich in images and metaphors, emotional, musical, dithyrambic, coloured by outlandish Gaelic turns:

As flies the unconstant sun, over Larmon's grassy hill; so pass the tales of old, along my soul, by night! When bards are removed to their place; when harps are hung in Selma's

hall; then comes a voice to Ossian, and awakes his soul!
It is the voice of years that are gone! they roll before me,
with all their deeds! I seize the tales, as they pass, and pour
them forth in song. Nor a troubled stream is the song of the
king, it is like the rising of music from Lutha of the strings.
Lutha of many strings, not silent are thy streamy rocks,
when the white hands of Malvina move upon the harp!
Light of the shadowy thoughts, that fly across my soul,
daughter of Toscar of helmets, wilt thou not hear the song!
We call back, maid of Lutha, the years that have rolled away!
(Opening lines of *Oina-Morul*)

Whatever our verdict as to their literary quality, whatever our
doubts as to their authenticity, the *Poems of Ossian* are of
historical importance in that they reveal what kind of poetry
fulfilled – and nurtured – Pre-Romantic aspirations. Moreover, they seemed to confirm the new view of poetry as the
spontaneous creation of a natural genius.

New aesthetics
Since the dissolution of the old Neo-classical system a new
theory of poetry had gradually been evolving. Dryden's and
Lessing's plea for the appreciation of beauties, Diderot's
'realism', Lessing's championship of Shakespeare as an
original genius all marked significant new starts. The key-
words 'genius', 'originality' and 'creation', as well as 'spontaneous' and 'natural' were in fact already current during the
Pre-Romantic period, as Logan Pearsall Smith has established
in his analysis of 'Four Romantic Words', in which he lists a
series of critical dissertations published between 1751 and 1774
by such writers as Joseph and Thomas Warton, Richard Hurd,
William Duff, Edmund Burke, William Sharpe on topics like
the genius of Pope, originality in authors, original genius, the
genius of Shakespeare, etc. Among these dull tracts ('the dusty
Saharas and Dead Seas of literature' in Smith's words), one

alone was of lasting interest: Young's *Conjectures on Original Composition* (1759). Not that Young's ideas were intrinsically novel; many attempts have indeed been made to prove the extent of his indebtedness to his predecessors. The *Conjectures* are none the less important because they summarize and crystallize the new lines of thought, stating them more cogently and more vividly than ever before. Young draws clear distinctions between imitation and originality, learning and genius, the rules and free creation, the ancients and the moderns:

> An original may be said to be of a vegetable nature, it rises spontaneously from the vital root of genius; it grows, it is not made; imitations are often a sort of manufacture wrought up by those mechanics, art and labour, out of pre-existent materials not their own.
>
> *(English Critical Essays XVI–XVIII Centuries.* London: Oxford Univ. Press, 1965, p. 274)

Young here even uses the image of organic growth subsequently favoured by Goethe and Coleridge. In his advocacy of an adventurous approach, his insistence on the divine inspiration of the genius, his emphasis on originality and spontaneity, and also in his vivid phraseology, Young was foreshadowing the poetic theory of the Romantics. The *Conjectures* are not a further amendment of the Neo-classical code in the manner of the Enlightenment; they are a replacement of the old with a new, in many ways antithetical set of notions.

The *Conjectures* had less immediate resonance in England than abroad, particularly in Germany, where the first translation in 1760 received prompt and wide attention. Young's aesthetic programme seemed tailor-made for the *Sturm und Drang (Storm and Stress)* movement of the early 1770s. These youthful writers – Goethe (1749–1832), Schiller (1759–1805),

Herder (1744–1803), Klinger (1752–1831), Lenz (1751–92), Bürger (1747–97) – were in rebellion against any organized creed, literary, social, political or religious. In their dynamic urge to break out of the bonds of the past, they rejected every facet of the *status quo*. All that mattered, in life as in art, was the original, creative genius of the individual who must be free to express his personal experience spontaneously. No wonder that the *Storm and Stress* is alternatively known as the 'Age of Genius'.

Thus once again in the spread of the new aesthetics, as in the sentimental novel, in the expression of melancholy and in the discovery of primitive poetry, the vital impetus during the Pre-Romantic period came from England, although many of these innovations had a greater and more rapid effect across the Channel than in their country of origin. The liberal English tradition of freedom to air one's views from any soap-box has always been conducive to a wealth of new ideas. On the other hand, this very freedom, together with a fine native literature, produced less need for radical reform than in Germany, where men were avid for a new start after a long stretch of relative sterility. The violence of the *Storm and Stress* and the extremism of the German Romantic movements reflect the desire to 'catch up' and indeed outdo others. In France there was a little of both these attitudes: immense pride in and loyalty to the indigenous Classical writers, mingled with a growing longing for something new and a curiosity about 'foreign' notions. In this way the pre-history of the Romantic movement not only elucidates the meaning of Romanticism as a whole, but already determines the character of individual Romantic groups.

3

The Romantics and their works

By the time the Romantic movement as such manifested itself with the formation of a group round the brothers Schlegel in Germany in the closing years of the eighteenth century and with the publication of Wordsworth's and Coleridge's *Lyrical Ballads* in 1798, many of the attitudes, ideas and styles associated with Romantic art had already appeared, at least in embryonic form. A fundamental re-orientation was taking place throughout the eighteenth century, as I have tried to show. In this sense the Romantic movement was the outcome and the culmination of a long process of evolution. But, paradoxical though it may sound, its slow development does not invalidate, or even contradict, the common conception of the advent of Romanticism as a revolution. It was both, in so far as the total effect of that evolution was revolutionary for it meant a reversal in theories of creation, in standards of beauty, in ideals and in modes of expression. Such radical changes as the break-through of Romanticism implied could not possibly have come other than as the result of a lengthy maturation.

The Romantic movement was a continuation of Pre-Romanticism, but it was more than that in one crucial point: its evaluation of the imagination. As Sir Maurice Bowra has pointed out in the first sentence of his collection of essays, *The Romantic Imagination*:

If we wish to distinguish a single characteristic which differentiates the English Romantics from the poets of the eighteenth century, it is to be found in the importance which they attached to the imagination and in the special view which they held of it.

The change from the eighteenth-century mimetic to the nineteenth- (and twentieth-) century expressive conception of the imagination has been brilliantly analysed by M. H. Abrams in *The Mirror and the Lamp*. During the Enlightenment there had been a nascent appreciation of the magical powers of the imagination, but the Pre-Romantics tended rather to emphasize naturalness, spontaneity, primitiveness. Only with the Romantics did imagination really come to the forefront. The subjective philosophy of Fichte certainly played a part in this through its contention that the very existence and shape of the world depended entirely on the vision of the individual imagination. The table or the tree is *because* and *as* we see it; or, as Blake put it when he was asked ' "When the Sun rises, do you not see a round disc of fire somewhat like a Guinea?" O no, no. I see an Innumerable company of the Heavenly host crying, "Holy, Holy, Holy is the Lord God Almighty" ' *(Vision of the Last Judgement* in *Complete Writings*, ed. G. Keynes, London: Oxford Univ. Press, 1966, p. 617). Blake adds the comment, 'I question not my Corporeal or Vegetative Eye any more than I would Question a Window concerning a Sight. I look through it and not with it.' What Blake and the Romantics look with is the eye of the imagination, which allows them to see beyond surface reality to the immanent ideal. They were keenly conscious of the chasm between the transient, commonsense world of appearances and the eternal, infinite realm of ideal truth and beauty, which man can perceive by means of the imagination. When Coleridge wrote in the *Dejection Ode*

> Ah! from the soul itself must issue forth
> A light, a glory, a fair luminous cloud

he was referring to what he called in a subsequent stanza

My shaping spirit of Imagination

the power that infuses meaning into 'that inanimate cold world'. Hence the power of the imagination forms one of the central themes of *Biographia Literaria*, as also of Shelley's *Defence of Poetry* where poetry is defined as 'the expression of the imagination' (*Complete Works*, ed. R. Ingpen and W. Beck, London: Benn, 1965, vol. vii, p. 109). Similarly Wordsworth spoke of poetry as 'works of imagination and sentiment' (*Poetical Works*, ed. E. de Selincourt, Oxford: Clarendon Press, 1944, vol. ii, p. 409) and Keats, in a letter to his brother George, 18 September 1819, wrote of himself: 'I describe what I imagine', a phrase that could well be the device of all truly Romantic art, whose highest function is to portray the world in such a way that the infinite in the finite, the ideal within the actual is unveiled in all its beauty.

This conception of the creative imagination is a more nearly reliable criterion of Romanticism than any other single factor. Byron did not subscribe to it, but then Byron has as many (if not more) affinities with the poets of the eighteenth century as with Coleridge, Shelley, Blake, Keats and Wordsworth. Nor did several of the so-called French Romantics grasp the central role of the imagination, but they are more akin to the iconoclastic, Pre-Romantic *Storm and Stress*, because developments in France were so retarded by the intervention of the Revolution and the persistence of Neo-classicism that the primacy of the imagination as the 'queen of all faculties' was fully recognized only by Baudelaire and the Symbolists in the mid-nineteenth century. The German Romantics, however, shared the beliefs of the English and often saw Blake's Heavenly host (and even stanger sights) when looking at the sun.

It is thus apparent that there is a certain interplay of similarities and differences among the European Romantics.

To go into this subject is beyond the scope of this monograph; conversely, to avoid it altogether would mean a simplification to the point of distortion. It might, therefore, be helpful at this stage to give a brief account of the various Romantic groups in chronological order. For in considering the Romantics, it is all too easy to forget how large a number of individual parts the movement compromised and also how great a time-span it covered.

The successive groups

The German Romantics

The German Romantics fall into two distinct generations known as the *Frühromantik* (the 'Early Romantics') and the *Hochromantik* (the 'High Romantics') or, sometimes, *die jüngere Romantik* ('the Younger Romantics'). The former is the first European Romantic group, dating from 1797 until the opening years of the nineteenth century. Its centre was for a short time Berlin, then the small university town of Jena, whence it derived its alternative name of *Jenaromantik*. Likewise, the second phase, from about 1810–20, is often called the *Heidelbergromantik*, although only some of its members met in Heidelberg; others were in Munich and Vienna. In spite of a certain continuity both of personalities and of ideas, the two generations are in many respects different in emphasis and in character. Thus even in the limited space of a national entity, it is difficult to generalize about 'the Romantics'.

The *Frühromantik* was very conscious of its coherence as a group, whose focal point was the brothers Schlegel: Friedrich (1759–1805), inventive but erratic, and August Wilhelm (1767–1845), whose more orderly turn of mind enabled him to transmit his brother's ideas and to act as the 'interpreter' of German Romantic theory in his lectures on the dramatic and the fine arts, which were translated into English and French in the

second decade of the nineteenth century. The Early Romantics'
esprit de corps was not in contradiction to Romantic individualism for it sprang in part from a belief in the importance
of the individual who could be approached through friendship,
through those curious communal activities based on the Greek
particle 'syn', meaning 'togetherness': 'Synexistenz', 'Sym-
philosophieren', 'Synenthusiasmus', 'Sympoesie', etc. In practice this involved the Early Romantics in dawn frog-catching
expeditions to supply experimental material for their scientist
members! For they were certainly extraordinarily catholic in
their interests which ranged from philosophy and poetry to
religion, statesmanship and the natural sciences. Hence the
group comprised not only the poets Wackenroder (1773–98),
Tieck (1773–1853) and Novalis (pseudonym of Hardenberg,
1772–1801), but also the religious thinker Schleiermacher, the
natural philosophers Schelling and Baader, and the physicist
Ritter. Nor was this universality merely a manifestation of the
traditional German mania for culture; it stemmed from a view
of Romanticism as a total existentialist revaluation that was to
radiate outwards from poetry to transform ('poeticize' was
their word) the whole world.

These beliefs were put forward in the large body of theoretical writings that are the Early Romantics' chief claim to fame.
With the exception of Novalis and Wackenroder, both of
whom died young, and of Tieck, who was somewhat ex-
traneous to the group, the Early Romantics were speculative
manipulators of ideas rather than creative poets. Their
tendency to metaphysical abstractions is amply illustrated by
Schleiermacher's *Versuch einer Theorie des geselligen Betragens
(Attempt at a theory of social behaviour)*, a sort of systematiza-
tion of friendship. Many of their ideas were couched in
aphoristic fragments which appeared in their journal, *Athenäum*. The revaluation of human existence began from the
standpoint of the utter subjectivism preached by Fichte. Since
the world depends on our perception, we can reshape it in a

constantly progressive, magical idealism. The means to perform this poeticization is the creative imagination, particularly that of the artist, who for this reason occupies the supreme place in this scheme. The work of art has a mediating function in that it portrays, in a symbolical approximation, the artist's vision of the transcendental realm to which his imagination gives him access. Obviously, no cursory summary of this kind can do justice to this intricate aesthetic, so largely dependent on intuition and so strongly tinged with pseudo-religious mysticism. Quite apart from the ideas, words (such as 'poetry', 'nature', 'longing', etc.) are frequently used in so esoteric a fashion as to enhance the difficulties of interpretation. A sample, Friedrich Schlegel's definition of Romantic poetry in Fragment 116 of the *Athenäum*, will be more revealing than any further comment:

> Die romantische Poesie ist eine progressive Universalpoesie. Ihre Bestimmung ist nicht bloss, alle getrennte Gattungen der Poesie wieder zu vereinigen und die Poesie mit der Philosophie und Rhetorik in Berührung zu setzen. Sie will und soll auch Poesie und Prosa, Genialität und Kritik, Kunstpoesie und Naturpoesie bald mischen, bald verschmelzen, die Poesie lebendig und gesellig und das Leben und die Gesellschaft poetisch machen, den Witz poetisieren und die Formen der Kunst mit gediegnem Bildungsstoff jeder Art anfüllen und sättigen und durch die Schwingungen des Humors beseelen. Sie umfasst alles, was nur poetisch ist vom grössten, wieder mehrere Systeme in sich enthaltenden Systeme der Kunst bis zu dem Seufzer, dem Kuss, den das dichtende Kind aushaucht in kunstlosen Gesang. Sie kann sich so in das Dargestellte verlieren, dass man glauben möchte poetische Individuen jeder Art zu charakterisieren, sei ihr eins und alles und doch gibt es noch keine Form, die dazu gemacht wäre, den Gseit des Autors vollständig auszudrücken: so dass manche Künstler, die nur auch

einen Roman schreiben wollten, von ungefähr sich selbst dargestellt haben. Nur sie kann gleich dem Epos ein Spiegel der ganzen umgebenden Welt, ein Bild des Zeitalters werden. Und doch kann auch sie am meisten zwischen dem Dargestellten und dem Darstellenden, frei von allem realen und idealen Interesse, auf den Flügeln der poetischen Reflexion in der Mitte schweben, diese Reflexion immer wieder potenzieren und wie in einer endlosen Reihe von Spiegeln vervielfachen. Sie ist der höchsten und der allseitigsten Bildung fähig, nicht bloss von innen heraus, sondern auch von aussen hinein, indem sie jedem, was ein Ganzes in ihren Produkten sein soll, alle Teile ähnlich organisiert, wodurch ihr die Aussicht auf eine grenzenlos wachsende Klassizität eröffnet wird. Die romantische Poesie ist unter den Künsten, was der Witz der Philosophie und die Gesellschaft, Umgang, Freundschaft und Liebe im Leben ist. Andre Dichtarten sind fertig und können nun vollständig zergliedert werden. Die romantische Dichtart ist noch im Werden; ja das ist ihr eigentliches Wesen, dass sie ewig nur werden, nie vollendet sein kann. Sie kann durch keine Theorie erschöpft werden, und nur eine divinatorische Kritik dürfte es wagen, ihr Ideal charakterisieren zu wollen. Sie allein ist unendlich, wie sie allein frei ist und das als ihr erstes Gesetz anerkennt, dass die Willkür des Dichters kein Gesetz über sich leide. Die romantische Dichtart ist die einzige, die mehr als Art und gleichsam die Dichtkunst selbst ist: denn in einem gewissen Sinn ist oder soll alle Poesie romantisch sein.

(Romantic poetry is a progressive universal poetry. It is destined not merely to reunite the separate genres of poetry and to link poetry to philosophy and rhetoric. It would and should also mingle and fuse poetry and prose, genius and criticism, artistic poetry and natural poetry, make poetry lively and sociable, and life and society poetic, poeticize wit, fill and saturate the forms of art with worthwhile subject-matter of every kind, animated by an upsurge of humour. It embraces all that is poetic, from the most stupendously complex system of art down to the sigh, the kiss uttered in artless song by the child creating its own poetry. It can so identify itself with what is being portrayed that one might well believe its sole aim was to characterize poetic individuals of every sort; nevertheless there is as yet no form designed fully to express the author's spirit: so that some artists, who only wanted to write a novel, have more or less portrayed themselves. Romantic poetry alone can, like the epic, become a mirror of the whole world, a picture of the age. At the same time, free of all real and ideal interest, it can also float on wings of poetic reflection between the portrayed and the portrayer, constantly reinforcing this reflection and multiplying it as in an unending series of mirrors. It has the potential of the highest, most manifold evolution, not only through outward expansion, but also through inward infiltration, for each thing destined to be a whole entity is organized uniformly in all its parts, whereby the prospect of a boundless, ever-growing classicism is opened up. Among the arts Romantic poetry is what wit is to philosophy, and what sociability, friendship and love are to life. Other types of poetry are complete and can now be thoroughly dissected. Romantic poetry is still in the process of creation; this indeed is its very essence, that it is eternally evolving, never completed. It cannot be exhausted by any theory, and only a divinatory criticism could dare to try to characterize its ideal. It alone is infinite, just as it alone is quite free, recognizing as its prime law that the poet's caprice brooks no law. Romantic poetry is the only type of poetry that is more than merely a type, and is in fact the very art of poetry in itself: for in a certain sense all poetry is or should be romantic.)

After the extreme idealism of the Early Romantics, the younger generation, without formally renouncing their elders' programme, quietly reverted to more practical concerns, and was in fact far more productive. The well-known works of German Romanticism – the lyrics and tales of Arnim (1781–1831), Brentano (1778–1842), Chamisso (1781–1838), Eichendorff (1788–1857), Fouqué (1777–1843), Heine (1797–1856), Hoffman (1776–1822), Mörike (1804–75), Rückert (1788–1866), Uhland (1787–1862) – all come from the High Romantics, who resumed and developed the interests of the Pre-Romantics: the fascination of the past, the cult of the natural and the simple, the exploration of the supernatural, and in poetic expression musicality and spontaneity. To this heritage they added a strong nationalistic bias which led to a scholarly investigation of the history of the German language (by the brothers Grimm) as well as to numerous collections of Germanic folk-songs and -tales. These served as a model for the High Romantics' own writings in which they aimed to recapture the naïvety of folk utterance in an apparently artless art.

The English Romantics

The English Romantics cannot be as neatly categorized as the Germans or even the French despite the efforts of some earlier critics. Herford, in *The Age of Wordsworth*, suggests the following division: the Wordsworth group of 1798–1806, centred on Stowey and Grasmere, comprising Coleridge, Crabbe and Clare, lofty in its emphasis on the harmony between nature and man; secondly, the Scott group of 1805–10, including Campbell, Moore and Southey, concentrating on medievalism and the Borderlands, steeped in tradition and finding its chief expression in narrative poetry; and finally the Shelley group of 1818–22, the cosmopolitans, such as Byron and Keats, equally at home in Italy and Greece, passionate in their assertion of freedom and beauty. Such a rigid classification is hardly illuminating for it begs more questions than it answers: is there any real affinity between Byron and Keats,

Coleridge and Clare? is Scott not as much a realist as a romantic? and what is the place of Blake in this scheme? Rather than
dissipate energy in the futile academic exercise of trying to
'pigeon-hole' poets, it is wiser – and truer – to admit at the
outset that 'in England, as opposed to the Continent, there was
no "romantic" movement, if we limit the meaning of such a
term to a conscious program and consider the precise name as
crucial' (R. Wellek, *History of Modern Criticism*, vol. ii, p. 110).
This is by no means intended as a criticism; on the contrary, in
its lack of cohesion lies the very strength of English Romanticism. For its outstanding trait is its individualism, and from
this stems its variety, its vigour and its freshness.

In answer to the question why English Romanticism
differed in this way from its Continental counterparts, it is
possible to suggest several tentative reasons. Invidious though
it is to speak of national character, there does seem to be a
marked streak of independence in the English mind which has
led to non-conformism. The French *Pléiade* and *Cénacle*, the
German *Göttinger Dichterbund* and *Frühromantik* really have
no equivalent in English literature as group endeavours. More
specifically, and probably more important, the English
Romantics were not forced together by any common cam-
paign, such as the French struggle against Neo-classicism and
the German ambition to develop a great national literature.
English Romanticism, in contrast, evolved gradually and
peacefully out of the new notions which had been infiltrating
gently throughout the later eighteenth century. So instead of
the aggressive momentum that unified the German and the
French Romantics, the English had a 'sense of belonging to
and restoring the native tradition' (N. Frye, *English Romantic
Poets*, p. 65). There was no real break in continuity, no violent
sense of revolution; in the poetry of Byron and Clare many
earlier elements persisted, while the novels of Scott, Peacock
and Jane Austen bear witness to the flourishing current of
realism during the early nineteenth century.

Romanticism in England was, therefore, informal and easy-going, 'a wam intuitive muddle', as H. N. Fairchild has called it in his brief but excellent survey in the symposium published in *PMLA* (vol. iv, 1940, p. 24). By this he means that the English Romantics were pragmatic rather than systematic in their philosophy, that they had no journals, programmes or theories such as abounded on the Continent – often, incidentally, to the detriment of creative writing, as among the German Early Romantics. It is significant that Keats scattered his aesthetic comments in his letters and that the manifestos of English Romanticism were, like Wordsworth's *Preface to the Lyrical Ballads*, Coleridge's *Biographia Literaria* and Shelley's *Defence of Poetry*, written *after* the poetry to which they refer back. These three works alone are evidence of the range and variety of English Romanticism; they have in common a lofty conception of poetry, an assertion of the powers of the imagination, a concern with poetic diction and with the relationship of the real to the ideal, but each is recognizably the expression of an individual approach. Thus English Romanticism can embrace both the realism of Wordsworth's adherence to nature and the idealism of Shelley's visionary transcendentalism. Because of its very freedom it produced a large number of suggestive critical ideas as well as a wealth of fine poetry.

The French Romantics
The French Romantics are chronologically the last; the first collection of poems in the new vein, Lamartine's *Méditations poétiques*, appeared in 1820, while the theatre was not conquered till 1830, the year of Hugo's *Hernani*. This tardiness is due to two factors which, together, were decisive in shaping French Romanticism: the one has already been noted, namely the persistence of the Neo-classical tradition; the other is the intervention of political events, particularly the Revolution of 1789. Nowhere else was the Romantic movement as inextric-

ably tied up in political (and religious) strife as in France. The effect of the Revolution is hard to assess with any certainty because such persuasive arguments can be put forward in support of various hypotheses. For instance, it can quite validly be said that the old absolute monarchy upheld authoritarianism in literature as well as in government so that its fall would topple Neo-classicism too, and indeed one of the mottoes of the time was: 'à société nouvelle, littérature nouvelle' ('for a new society, a new literature'). It was not, however, so simple: the atmosphere of fear during the Reign of Terror was hardly conducive to the discussion of new ideas which might easily cost one's head – hence that strange hiatus, the period of virtual silence from 1790 till 1820. Napoleon's accession as Emperor brought a further set-back when he inaugurated a revival of the old ideal of orderliness in his admiration for military virtues. A final complication is the misguided patriotism which led Napoleon and the French to regard the *ancien régime* in literature as the jewel of their national heritage, the symbol of their cultural dominance in Europe. Consequently all foreign importations – and the innovations of Pre-Romanticism came largely from England and Germany – were distrusted as a threat to the glory of France. For this reason Mme de Staël's *De l'Allemagne (About Germany*, 1810) had to be published in England while Constant added a cautious preface to his translation of Schiller's *Wallenstein* even though it appeared in Geneva.

These background problems not only retarded the advent of Romanticism in France; they also help to explain the acrimonious conflict that surrounded its eventual emergence. The battle has been recorded blow by blow, almost day by day by R. Bray in his *Chronologie du romantisme* so that there is no need to go into details here. In essence it was a struggle between the die-hard, patriotic traditionalists, often Royalist in politics and Catholic in religion on the one hand, and on the other, the cosmopolitan progressives, who tended to be liberals in every facet of their views. Not that the division was always clear-cut; for a while, for example about 1822, there were Royalist Romantics and Liberal Romantics–as well as Classical Royalists and Classical Liberals! The groupings in the *salons* changed as rapidly as the journals *(Le Conservateur littéraire, Mercure du XIXième siècle, Débats, Muse française, Le Globe)*. Only when the warring factions of Romantics made peace among themselves, when the Left and the Right Wing rallied to Hugo's *Cénacle* in 1827 could the breakthrough be accomplished. A further impetus came in 1828 from Sainte-Beuve's *Tableau historique et critique de la poésie française et du théâtre français au XVIième siècle* which, by drawing parallels between the practices of the *Pléiade* and those of the *Cénacle*, gave the French Romantics a respectable ancestry in their native tradition.

The difficulties which the French Romantics had to combat determined their ideas to a considerable extent. In their barn-storming iconoclasm they are reminiscent of the German *Storm and Stress*, and their literary ideals are also similar in so far as both were fundamentally protest movements. Thus in opposition to the old dictum of Pascal that 'le moi est haïssable' ('the ego is hateworthy'), the French Romantics emphasized the role of feeling, expressed as spontaneously and passionately as possible. In revolt against the old artificial conventions, they repeatedly pleaded for truth and naturalness in dramatic structure and speech. Even Hugo's advocacy of the grotesque is conceivably a reversal of the former exclusive cult of harmonious beauty.

But in spite of all their excited energy, the French Romantics were not such bold innovators as they fancied. Their gaze was largely orientated backwards, to the kind of writing against which they were reacting. With the possible exception of Vigny, they had little genuine appreciation of the creative imagination so that their reforms amounted to a technical liberalization of verse and drama. This is perhaps what

Baudelaire meant when he commented that the French Romantics had sought salvation in outer factors rather than in the inner world. It was left to him in France to grasp the full significance of the inner world of the imagination.

The works

Few periods in literary history have, in a comparable time-span, produced as great an array of works as the Romantic movement. To give a critical survey of this wealth of writing is not the intention of this monograph, nor indeed would it be possible within the very limited space. But Romanticism was more than a mere concept or critical term; the re-orientation in aesthetics, particularly the release of the creative imagination and of individual feeling paved the way for a tremendous upsurge of new writing throughout Europe between about 1798 and 1832. These two aspects of the Romantic movement – the renewal in aesthetics and in writing – are closely interrelated in that the theoretical revaluation preceded, accompanied and also fashioned the forms of poetic expression, as becomes evident from an examination of the three literary genres.

The lyric

The lyric is undoubtedly the chief glory of the Romantic movement. During this period it achieved a freedom, a flexibility and an intensity rarely equalled and certainly never surpassed. Because of its very wide range and its excellence, however, it is the form least amenable to the generalizations of a monograph such as this. The voice in the Romantic lyric is, above all, a highly individual voice, and to do it justice, requires individual analysis. To speak of the qualities of the Romantic lyric (in a few hundred words!) is almost as disheartening a task as to seek a definition of Romanticism, and for much the same reasons.

In the Romantic aesthetics there were certain factors which

clearly encouraged the development of the lyric. First and foremost among these is the new conception of the imagination as a creative, transforming force, central to the artistic process. Nowhere perhaps was this to have a more immediately apparent effect than in the lyric. No longer was the world described with what Blake called the 'corporeal eye' and the sober words turned into 'poetry' by the addition of some pretty similes, as even Gray had suggested to a pupil. The Romantic poet drew instead on his vision of the Heavenly host, to refer again to Blake's vital distinction between the real and the visionary. This does not imply that the Romantics disregarded reality; indeed, few English poets have been more keenly appreciative of the natural world than Wordsworth and Keats. But the Romantic is at the same time also always aware of the immanence of the ideal in the real, the Heavenly host as well as the golden guinea of fire when he sees the sun. Wordsworth, for instance, perceives the underlying significance of the daffodils or of the leech-gatherer besides their surface appearance. Similarly Keats in the *Ode to Autumn*, Shelley in his dirge *Autumn*, Lamartine in *L'Automne*, Eichendorff and Lenau in a whole series of lyrics, all suggest the inner essence of autumn as each conceives it, whereas earlier writers, both in England and on the Continent, had largely concentrated on its outer manifestations. The balance between the real and the visionary varies, of course, from poet to poet: from the marked element of realistic observation in Wordsworth to the primacy of the imaginative in Coleridge's surrealistic *Kubla Khan*, *Christabel* and *The Ancient Mariner*. But whatever the balance, there is a fundamental tension between the real and the transcendental, and it is this which gives the Romantic lyric its peculiarly haunting quality.

This constant awareness of the immanece of the ideal has a direct effect on the Romantics' poetic technique too. For one of their cardinal problems was how to make the ideal real in their works, how to express the inward and abstract by the outward and concrete. To this problem A. W. Schlegel offered a solution when he maintained that the transcendental could become apparent 'nur symbolisch, in Bildern und Zeichen' ('only symbolically, in images and signs') *(Vorlesung über schöne Kunst und Literatur*, ed. J. Minor, Heilbronn: Henninger, 1884, p. 91). Symbolical images thus assumed a vital, central role in Romantic poetry as the outer, visible vehicles of the inner visionary perception, in Coleridge's words, 'the living educts of the Imagination' (*Statesman's Manual* in *Political Tracts*, ed. R. J. White, Cambridge: Cambridge Univ. Press, 1953, p. 25) characterized 'above all by the translucence of the eternal through and in the temporal' (*Biographia Literaria*, ed. J. Shawcross, Oxford: Clarendon Press, 1907, vo. ii, p. 259). The function of the image changed radically from its early eighteenth-century peripheral place in the poem as a form of decoration to its commanding status in Romantic poetry as the operative carrier of meaning. There is no clearer example of such use of imagery than Blake's *Songs of Innocence* and *Songs of Experience* in which the quintessential idea is brilliantly distilled into a web of pregnant images.

> O Rose, thou art sick!
> The invisible worm,
> That flies in the night,
> In the howling storm,
> Has found out thy bed
> Of crimson joy;
> And his dark secret love
> Does thy life destroy.

This horrifying picture of *The Sick Rose* tells us more, in a wholly metaphorical manner, about the state of 'experience' than any amount of explicit comment. For this reason, because it is in fact the only way to convey something of their imaginative vision, the Romantics had continual recourse to symbolic images which range from the common, relatively transparent ones of the harp as the emblem of the poetic process throughout Coleridge or 'the correspondent breeze' in Shelley, Coleridge, Wordsworth and Byron as a sign of spiritual activism,[1] to the esoteric images of Blake's or Novalis's later work. In this central focus on the symbolic image, Romanticism brought an innovation of far-reaching importance for the subsequent development of poetry. The Romantics laid the foundations for the modern lyric of suggestion and had already produced some of its finest examples.

Apart from the new conception of the nature and function of the imagination, two further elements fostered the Romantic lyric. Both have their origins in the Pre-Romantic period and have already been discussed in that context: the cult of feeling and the quest for the natural. In the Romantic lyric these two features took on a special meaning. The stock emotionalism of the Age of Sentiment, as exemplified in the stilted extravagance of many novels of sensibility, was replaced by the individual's personal feeling, or, as Lamartine put it, the conventional lyre of Parnassus gave way to the strings of the human heart. This is particularly marked in France, where personal emotion had been severely kept in check by the smooth objectivity for which Neo-classicism had aimed. The undue stress on the subjective in both the theory and the practice of the French Romantic poets is undoubtedly part of the reaction against the old creed, but this exaltation of feeling could all too easily lead to a certain theatrical quality, a self-melodramatization in grandiloquent rhetoric. In England too poetry was regarded as 'the spontaneous overflow of powerful feelings', to quote Wordsworth's famous phrase from the *Preface to the Lyrical Ballads*. But in actual fact there

[1] See M. H. Abrams' interesting analysis of this image in *English Romantic Poets*, pp. 37–54.

was little vehement 'overflow' for emotion was not only 'recollected in tranquillity' but controlled by various factors: in Byron by the mocking note of irony, in Keats by the overriding 'sense of Beauty', in Wordsworth by the observation of the outer world, and always by the use of imagery as an objective correlative that conveys, and yet at the same time, restrains feeling. A comparison between Lamartine's *L'Automne* and Keat's *Ode to Autumn* well illustrates the difference between the totally subjective approach of the French and the more objective tendency of the English; Lamartine's poem is an intensely personal elegy, centred exclusively on his own mood which nature merely serves to reflect, whereas Keats gives an evocation of the season, at once realistic and so highly imaginative as to transfigure his own emotion. In Germany the decisive assertion of feeling had already occurred in the Storm and Stress of the 1770s so that the Romantics had less need to place explicit emphasis on it although their lyrics certainly pulsate with emotion.

The pursuit of the natural was also important in shaping the Romantic lyric and it affected both subject-matter and language. In contrast to the elegance and wit of the Augustans, Wordsworth maintained that the poet should 'choose incidents and situations from common life' and relate them 'as far as was possible, in a selection of language really used by men'. There was wide agreement among the English Romantics particularly on this latter point, the need to use the familiar language of men in place of a stylized, peculiar poetic diction. The impact of the English Romantic lyric derives from the striking combination of simplicity with suggestive imagery. The French, in spite of their clamour for truthfulness and naturalness, found it much harder to free themselves from their traditional oratory, traces of which surely lurk in their liking for antithesis, enumeration, rhetorical questions and fine phrases. In Germany it was the High Romantics who sought the natural after the metaphysical complexities of the

Early Romantics. They consciously modelled their lyrics on the folk-songs which they collected with such enthusiasm, and they were indeed remarkably successful in capturing their atmosphere in the ballad-like lyrics that tell in direct, unadorned, musical language of millers, shepherds, soldiers, wanderers, mothers at the cradle and maidens at the spinning-wheel.

The narrative

The narrative was most cultivated by the Germans. F. Schlegel's *Gespräch über die Poesie (Conversation about Poetry* 1800), included a 'Brief über den Roman' ('Letter about the Novel'), which makes it clear that he invested the word *Roman* – the standard German term for 'novel' – with a special meaning. Connecting *Roman* directly with *romantisch*, he maintained that the narrative was *the* Romantic form. But to F. Schlegel and his fellow German Romantics, a *Roman* did not mean what we generally understand by 'novel'; it seems more to approximate to the total work of art later attempted by Wagner, for it was said to embrace prose and poetry, the narrative, the lyrical and the dramatic in one grandiosely comprehensive work. The eccentricity of this view is brought out by the reference to Shakespeare's plays as proto-types of the *Roman*! Bizarre though it is, F. Schlegel's theory helps in approaching the highly unconventional narratives of the German Romantics. Often tenuous in plot and shadowy in characterization, held together, not always successfully, by a theme or a mood, these works seem at times to foreshadow more recent experiments with the form of the novel. F. Schlegel's own *Lucinde* (1799), a string of thirteen sections about the relationship of Lucinde to Julius, interspersed with an 'Allegory on Impudence' and an 'Idyll on Idleness', though branded a 'non-novel' ('ein Unroman') by his brother, in spite of its undeniable weaknesses, certainly represents a bold departure in its structural organization. Similarly, Wackenroder's *Herzensergiessungen eines kunstliebenden Kloster-bruders (Outpourings from the heart of an art-loving friar*, 1797) is a loose collection of nineteen pieces all concerned with the holiness of art, all rhapsodical in tone. In Novalis's *Heinrich von Ofterdingen* (1802) too the scant outer plot increasingly recedes before the inner theme, the development of Heinrich into a poet and the progressive poeticization of the world. In its drift into a dream world *Heinrich von Ofterdingen* illustrates another type of narrative much favoured by both the Early and the High Romantics: the *Märchen*. The dictionary equivalent for this term is 'fairy-tale', but by *Märchen* the German Romantics really denoted any tale that entered into the realm of the imagination. Hence their strong preference for this genre with its musical form of composition and its scope for individual phantasy. In such *Märchen* as Novalis's *Hyazinth und Rosenblütchen (Hyacinth and Rosebud)*, in *Die Lehrlinge zu Sais (The Apprentices at Sais*, 1802), Fouqué's *Undine* (1811), Chamisso's *Peter Schlemihl* (1814) and the many tales of Hoffmann, German Romanticism finds its most distinctive, and often its best expression.

In the main, however, the Romantic narrative tended to concentrate in two areas: the 'confessional' and the historical. The former is patently indebted to the eighteenth-century sentimental novel in its use of the narrative as a vehicle for the exploration of emotion. The shift of emphasis to personal feeling is as evident in the novel as in lyric poetry, and it received a strong impetus from Rousseau's *Confessions* (1781) with its avowed programme of showing men 'un homme dans toute la vérité de la nature; et cet homme, ce sera moi' ('a man wholly true to nature; and this man will be myself'). 'Moi seul' ('myself alone'), Rousseau repeats in order to stress the auto-biographical element, which was to become a salient feature of Romantic writing. De Quincey's *Confessions of an English Opium-Eater* (1821), Wordsworth's *Prelude* (1805) and Byron's *Childe Harold's Pilgrimage* (1812) are all 'confessional' in character. So are most of the works that portray the Romantic 'hero', although the autobiographical origins may be more or less veiled. From Goethe's *Werther* (1774), through Chateaubriand's *Atala* (1801) and *René* (1805) Ugo Foscolo's *Ultime lettere di Jacopo Ortis* (1802) and Sénancour's *Obermann* (1804), to Musset's *Confession d'un enfant du siècle* (1836) – and, peripherally, Byron's *Don Juan* (1819–24) – this type of narrative was much in favour.

Its success was equalled only by that of the historical novel which was nurtured by the Romantic interest in the past. Not that the past was reproduced with much pretence at historical accuracy in most of these works: Hugo's *Notre-Dame de Paris* (1831) or Tieck's *Franz Sternbalds Wanderungen* (1798), for instance, give only the haziest, highly-coloured evocation of idealized 'good olde tymes'. On the other hand, Scott was often considerably more realistic, particularly at his best in such novels as *Waverley* (1814), *Rob Roy* (1817) and *The Heart of Midlothian* (1818), set in the fairly recent past of his native Scotland. This was probably sufficiently remote to satisfy the thirst for the distant on the Continent, where Scott enjoyed tremendous popularity.

The drama

The dramatic was the genre which, by and large, fared worst during the Romantic period. 'The age we live in,' Hazlitt wrote in the *London Magazine* of April 1820, 'is critical, didactic, paradoxical, romantic, but it is not dramatic.' The very principles on which lyric poetry could thrive – the caprice of the subjective imagination and the freedom of emotional expression – were basically inimical to the demands of drama, the most objective and also the most disciplined of literary forms. The finite shape of a successful acting play stands at the opposite pole to the expansive modes favoured by the Romantics. For this reason there is a marked dearth of dramatic production in the early years of the nineteenth century in spite of the manifold theatrical opportunities. The so-called 'popular' theatre found an outlet in melodrama, which may well have flourished for lack of anything better. This is one of the two categories into which Herford divides the drama of the age of Wordsworth: 'plays which are not literature', the other being 'literary exercises which are not in the fullest sense plays' (*Age of Wordsworth*, p. 135). In this latter phrase he is referring to works such as Byron's *Manfred* (1817) and *Cain* (1821), or Shelley's *Prometheus Unbound* (1820) and *Hellas* (1822), dramatized poems that present a static series of situations without any real dramatic tension or conflict. The lyrical element is so over-dominant as to make these 'plays' quite unsuitable for the stage, and this is equally true of the complex arabesques of an imagination running riot in Tieck's dramatic attempts. No wonder that barely a quarter of the plays in the first three decades of the nineteenth century were ever performed (see P. van Tieghem, *Le Romantisme dans la littérature européenne*, p. 445). This indeed is, as Herford already recognized, 'the one region of letters in which Romanticism failed' (Herford, p. 135), with very few exceptions such as Shelley's *The Cenci* (1819); certainly Coleridge is not remembered for *Remorse* (1813) nor Keats for *Otho the Great* (1819).

Only in France was drama central to the Romantic movement. This is because French Romanticism was to such a large extent inspired by opposition to the Neo-classical tradition, which was at its most potent in the theatre. Long after the new ideas and styles had infiltrated into prose with Rousseau and Bernardin de Saint-Pierre and had even become acceptable in lyric poetry with Lamartine's *Méditations poétiques* (1820), the battle continued in drama, and in fact this last fortress, this literary Bastille, as it was called, did not fall till the uproarious triumph of Hugo's *Hernani* in 1830. The ideals and practices of French Romantic drama were predominantly negative in origin, stemming from a reaction against all that had hitherto been obligatory: the strict observance of the three unities, the anonymous settings, the use of high-flown verse, the meticulous division into tragedy and comedy, the avoidance of violent action on the stage and hence the dependence on *récit* (literally 'recital', i.e. of crucial happenings off-stage). Instead of these conventions French Romantic drama took Shakespeare as its model in its mingling of the tragic and the comic, verse and prose, its disregard for the unities, its cult of picturesque 'local colour', its greater vigour in both speech and action in an attempt to fulfil the French Romantics' demand for truthfulness and naturalness.

4
Problems

In the face of this galaxy of works and of poets pertaining to the Romantic movement – not to mention Leopardi (1798–1837), Manzoni (1785–1873) and Foscolo (1778–1827) in Italy, Espronceda (1808–42) in Spain, Mickiewicz (1798–1855) and Slowacki (1809–49) in Poland, Pushkin (1799–1837) and Lermontov (1814–41) in Russia, Petöfi (1823–49) in Hungary, Oehlenschläger (1799–1850) in Denmark, Melville (1819–91) in America – it becomes evident why it is not possible to formulate a single, simple definition of Romanticism that would satisfactorily embrace all the writers associated with it. To the contention that 'he who seeks to define Romanticism is entering a hazardous occupation' a rider could be added to the effect that he who has some understanding of the meaning of Romanticism ceases to expect or to seek a neat dictionary definition. It lies in the nature of Romanticism that any study of it should lead to an awareness of its inherent problems rather than to the sort of absolute conclusions that would allow us to close the book on Romanticism once and for all. Its extraordinary wealth of poetic works, its wide spread both geographically and historically, its great range of interests and techniques undoubtedly encourage a continuing pre-occupation with the Romantic movement. But the fundamental reason for its endless fascination resides in its very essence: in abandoning the certainties of Rationalism, Romanticism threw the doors wide open to searching of every kind, in aesthetics, in metaphysics, in religion, in politics and social sciences as well as in literary expression. It is a movement that begs questions, questions that are often without answer.

This perhaps accounts for the fact that few areas of literary history have provoked as much discussion as Romanticism. The problem of definition is only one of several controversies that have raged for decades and still incense those who try to grapple with them. In lieu of a conclusion that would in any case be only tentative, it is therefore more fitting to end with a short review of some of the chief loci of contention.

Unity or diversity?

If we examine the characteristics of the actual literature which called itself or was called 'romantic' all over the continent, we find throughout Europe the same conceptions of poetry and of the workings and nature of the poetic imagination, the same conception of nature and its relation to man, and basically the same poetic style, with a use of imagery, symbolism, and myth which is clearly distinct from that of eighteenth-century neoclassicism.

(R. Wellek, 'The Concept of Romanticism',
Concepts of Criticism, pp. 160–1)

. . . any study of the subject should begin with a recognition of a *prima-facie* plurality of Romanticisms.

(A. O. Lovejoy, 'On the Discrimination
of Romanticisms', *English Romantic Poets*, p. 9)

These two statements represent the two sides in the argument as to the unity or diversity of Romanticism, and by one of those paradoxes not infrequent in connection with this movement, both are in fact true. More emphasis has been put in comparative studies on the unity of European Romanticism, perhaps to counteract the fragmentation wrought by increasingly specialized scrutiny of a particular aspect of a single poet. The attempt to achieve a synthesis is best exemplified by P. van Tieghem's panoramic survey, *Le Romantisme dans la littérature européenne*, which brings together certain dominant features of Romantic writing in a large number of literatures. This concept of a pan-European Romanticism has since been fostered by Wellek, who bases his case on the palpable difference between the practices and views of the Romantics and those of their predecessors. His arguments on the distinction between the imagery of Pope and Shelley, Lessing and Novalis, Voltaire and Hugo are incontrovertible (*Concepts of Criticism*, pp. 196–7); but when he uses this point to refute Lovejoy's plea for the discrimination of Romanticisms, the logic is questionable.

Herein, it seems to me, lies the fallacy of the 'synthesizing' approach: that from the existence of certain unmistakable similarities, it goes on – wrongly – to deduce an overall unity that is belied by the very varied faces of European Romanticism. This is not to deny, or even to belittle, the many fundamental recurrent qualities of Romantic art such as its individualism, its idealism, the primacy of the creative imagination, the subjective perception of nature, the importance of feeling, the use of symbolic imagery, etc. From these similarities stems that enigmatic family likeness of which we are vaguely aware in the products of Romanticism. But just as the members of a family may share certain common features without being identical, so the works of the Romantic movement bear its imprint, and yet still remain quite distinctive. The poetry of Wordsworth differs from that of Blake or of Lamartine or of Eichendorff; each belongs to the Romantic family and at the same time each is highly individual. Such examples could easily be multiplied from every field of Romantic endeavour to illustrate the interplay of unity and diversity. I have discussed this more fully in *Romanticism in Perspective*.

The relationship of 'romantic' to 'classical' and to 'realistic'

The problematic relationship of 'romantic' to 'classical' and to 'realistic' is a corollary of the difficulty in defining these terms. Since there is so little agreement about the meaning of 'romantic', it is natural that there should also be varying views as to its true antithesis. Both 'classical' and 'realistic' figure in literary and art criticism as the opposite of 'romantic'.

'Classical' is indeed almost as perplexing a word as 'romantic', as is fully admitted by those who contrast the two. Praz, for instance, sets them off against each other as 'symbols of specific tendencies of sensibility' (*Romantic Agony*, p. 34). Similarly, in his *Background of English Literature*, Grierson envisages them as 'a recurrent sequence of tendencies' (p. 256), 'the systole and diastole of the human heart in history' (p. 287); to him Romanticism 'represents men's dreams' (p. 289) in works in which 'the spirit counts for more than the form' (p. 261), while Classicism 'represents a synthesis, a balance' (p. 270) and as such has 'perfection of form' (p. 261). It is, I think, valid to argue that if Classicism is the perfect state of balanced harmony, it must needs embrace an element of Romanticism too; in other words, that Classicism, as the ideal synthesis, comprises the two extremes of Romanticism and Realism, and therefore is not really the opposite of Romanticism. This in no way invalidates the contention that the Romantic movement evolved partly in reaction to the Neo-classicism of the seventeenth century. Grierson's interpretation of 'classical' as denoting 'a balance' is obviously not pertinent to Neo-classicism with its strong bias towards the rational. The true inner spirit of ancient Classicism had been lost by the seventeenth century, as was evident from the often uncomprehending attempts at a rigid imitation of its outer forms. It is this Neo-classicism which many critics have in mind when they oppose 'classical' and 'romantic'. For example, when Pierre Moreau examines *Le Classicisme des roman-*

tiques (Paris: Plon, 1932), he is referring to the persistence of Neo-classical poetic practices in the writings of the Romantics.

If the relationship to 'classical' looks backwards to the Romantic movement's antecedents, the contrast with 'realistic' is mainly concerned with its successors. Realism – both as a facet of human temperament and in the literary sense – implies a primary interest in *res*, the thing as it is. In the arts realism purports to observe and depict all aspects of life as faithfully and factually as possible. Whether such objectivity is a viable artistic principle is another question. As a concept it is the radical antithesis of that idealism, that transformation through the subjective imagination that is the creed of Romanticism. In the light of this fundamental antagonism between the two approaches, it is tempting to portray the early nineteenth century as a period of Romanticism followed by a swing to the opposite pole of Realism. Tempting, but no more than partially true. The Romantic movement did lose much of its momentum after about 1830, and its excesses, as well as its achievements, led younger writers to seek new paths more in keeping with the sobriety of the rising middle-classes in an increasingly industrial civilization. But there are realistic streaks in Romantic writing too, admittedly less in Germany than in England and France, where 'truth to nature' – in the description of external reality and in the drama respectively – were highly esteemed. In practice the distinction between 'romantic' and 'realistic' is more fluid than critical theory would suggest. The fusion of 'realistic' and 'romantic' is as apparent in the Romantic poet, Wordsworth, as in the Realistic novelist, Flaubert.

The after-effects of Romanticism

Although the Romantic movement as such had lost most of its original impetus before the middle of the nineteenth century when it was superseded by Realism as the dominant mode, its ideas and styles were by no means extinct. For a time, it is true, Romantic attitudes fell into disfavour and not infrequently became the objects of ridicule. The Realists' and the Naturalists' emphasis on the careful observation and faithful reproduction of reality was clearly inimical to the Romantic principle of transformation through the creative imagination. But soon these quasi-photographic aims of the Realistic doctrine proved untenable for it was evident that the artist's imagination could not be excluded from his work, even if it was given another name. Zola, for instance, while insisting that the modern artist must proceed like the scientist in his attention to detail and his meticulous documentation, none the less conceded that art was reality 'seen through a temperament', as he put it. The individual temperament, however, inevitably gave *its* subjective view of reality rather than an objective copy. This is well illustrated in the evolution of the Impressionist painters, who began by observing scenes from contemporary life (in contrast to the historical and mythological subjects popular till then) and who came more and more not to reproduce what was before them, but to give a personal impression of what they saw in the play of light and colour. And Gauguin, as recent research has revealed, depicted less the Tahiti of his day than the paradise of his dreams.

The late nineteenth century thus brought a recrudescence of Romanticism. Hence the term 'Neo-romanticism' is sometimes used, particularly in German literature to refer to such poets as Hofmannsthal, George and the young Rilke. In Symbolism the heritage of Romanticism is apparent in the metaphysical conception of the universe existing in and through the poet, in the idealistic cult of beauty, in the mystical belief in a transcendental realm beyond appearances and in the attempts to convey the poet's perceptions in symbols. In technique as well as in outlook Symbolism is an elaboration of Romanticism, and the same claim is being made of Surrealism with its exploration of the subconscious. Indeed it can be argued that much of the writing of the twentieth century is in the wake of Romanticism; its anarchic individualism, ebullient imaginativeness and emotional vehemence were certainly implicit in the more extreme manifestations of the Romantic movement which offers precedents also for the search for new forms and symbols, the experimentation with time and place, the preference for an organic structure dependent on an associative fabric of recurrent images, the re-interpretation of myths, all considered characteristic of our century.

Whether the after-effects of Romanticism add up to a disruption or a regeneration of the European tradition is a matter of opinion. Some critics (notably I. Babbitt in *Rousseau and Romanticism*) have espoused Goethe's view of Romanticism as a sickness, a catastrophic misdirection that has allowed a self-indulgent *laissez-faire* to triumph over the discipline of genuine spiritual effort. In the arts, according to this school of thought, Romanticism eventually led to chaos masquerading as self-expression with a total contempt for form: action painting, novels printed on cards to be read in any chance order, indeterminate music that leaves the choice of notes to the performer. The darker, negative aspects of Romanticism undeniably come to fruition not only in the so-called Decadent movement of the late nineteenth and early twentieth centuries, but also, more subtly and insiduously, in the awareness of nothingness, nil, *le néant*, that has confronted man with increasing insistency since the failure to realize Romanticism's high ideals. This is one line of thought strongly represented in recent critical thinking. Of opposite view are those (J. Barzun, *Classic, Romantic and Modern;* M. Peckham, *Beyond the Tragic Vision*) who envisage Romanticism as a great period of reconstruction following the collapse of the old standards, as the harbinger of a greater flexibility in form, of freedom to experiment, of an organic and imaginative vision of the universe, which opened up any number of exciting vistas and possibilities. What is so remarkable about this controversy is that both camps admit the relevance of Romanticism to the art of today either as an evil or as a good force depending on their evaluation of its after-effects.

Moreover, the liveliness of the debate shows how potent Romanticism still is, and also how important an understanding of it is for the appreciation of nineteenth- and twentieth-century art. The break-through of the Romantic movement implied a fundamental re-orientation in aesthetics and it inspired a marvellous renewal in creative writing. It was a most fruitful movement in that it produced some of the finest works in European literature; and in so far as its notions and practices are still challenging today, it has been far-reaching in its significance.

Further Reading

Bibliographies

FOGLE, Richard H., *Romantic Poets and Prose Writers* (Golden-tree Bibliographies). New York: Appleton-Century-Crofts, 1967.
Comprehensive bibliographies for the British Romantic poets and prose writers and for the historical, aesthetic, social and intellectual backgrounds.

JORDAN, Frank, Jr. (ed.), *The English Romantic Poets. A Review of Research and Criticism*. 3rd. ed. New York: MLA, 1972.
Review of critical works on each of the English Romantic poets and on the movement as a whole.

WELLEK, René, 'Romanticism re-examined', in *Concepts of Criticism*. New Haven: Yale Univ. Press, 1963, pp. 199–221.
Invaluable for its assessment of critical works 1945–62.

Journals

Romantisme. Revue de la Société des Etudes Romantiques. 1971–
Studies in Romanticism. 1961–

Historical and social background

HAMPSON, Norman, *The First European Revolution, 1776–1815*. London: Thames & Hudson, 1969.
A lively presentation of the French Revolution in its European and cultural context.

JONES, Howard Mumford, *Revolution and Romanticism*. Cambridge: Harvard Univ. Press, 1974.
A stimulating presentation of the American and French Revolutions in their relationship to the Romantic ideology.

LAVER, James, *The Age of Illusion. Manners and Morals 1750–1848*. New York: McKay, 1972.
An exciting and well-illustrated study of social conditions that gives a vivid picture of domestic arrangements, religion, crime, pleasures and pastimes, etc.

TALMON, Jacob I., *Romanticism and Revolt: Europe 1815–1848*. London: Thames & Hudson, 1967.
A most illuminating, many-sided analysis of the changes in the European scene.

History and definition of 'romantic'

ABERCROMBIE, Lascelles, *Romanticism*. London: Secker, 1926.
A good starting-point; a sensible attempt to arrive at a fundamental understanding of the concept's meaning in the broadest sense.

BALDENSPERGER, Fernand, '"Romantique", ses analogues et ses équivalents: tableau synoptique de 1650 à 1810', *Harvard Studies and Notes in Philology*, 19 (1937), pp. 13–105.
A table of quotations illustrating the development of the word and the concept.

BARZUN, Jacques, *Classic, Romantic and Modern*. Garden City, N.Y.: Doubleday, 1961.
A most provocative book that offers an original definition of Romanticism, but one so wide as to be fraught with dangers.

EICHNER, Hans (ed.), '*Romantic' and its Cognates/The European History of a Word*. Toronto: Univ. of Toronto Press, 1972.
Essays by various contributors on the history of the term in England, France, Germany, Italy, Spain, Russia and Scandinavia; a mine of information.

GRIERSON, Herbert J. C., 'Classical and Romantic' in *The Background of English Literature*. London: Chatto & Windus, 1925.
An examination of these terms as denoting tendencies that recur throughout history.

JOST, François, 'A Lesson in a Word: "Romantic" and European Romanticism' in *Introduction to Comparative Literature*. Indianapolis and New York: Bobbs-Merrill, 1974, pp. 88–108.
Excellent in its documentation.

LOVEJOY, Arthur O., 'On the Discrimination of Romanticisms', *Publications of the Modern Language Asociation of America*, 39 (1924), pp. 229–53.
Presents the argument against the assumption of a sweeping uniformity in Romanticism; because of its importance reprinted in various collections, including Abrams' *English Romantic Poets*.

SMITH, Logan Pearsall, 'Four Romantic Words' in *Words and Idioms*. 4th ed. London: Constable, 1933. pp. 66–134.
Most illuminating enquiry into the origins and meaning of 'romantic', 'originality', 'creation' and 'genius'.

WELLEK, René, 'The concept of Romanticism in literary history', in *Concepts of Criticism*. New Haven: Yale Univ. Press, 1963, pp. 128–98.
Defines Romanticism by its common factors and insists on on the movement's basic unity throughout Europe.

General and European studies

ABRAMS, Meyer H., *The Mirror and the Lamp*. New York: Oxford Univ. Press, 1953.
A brilliant analysis of the contrast between the eighteenth-century mimetic and the nineteenth-century expressive theory of art.

BOWRA, Maurice, *The Romantic Imagination*. London: Oxford Univ. Press, 1950.
A volume of perceptive essays on specific works and poets; the first ('The Romantic Imagination') and the last ('The Romantic Achievement') are particularly valuable.

FRYE, Northrop (ed.), *Romanticism Reconsidered*. New York: Columbia Univ. Press, 1963.
A collection of essays by various hands, including M. H. Abrams' interesting analysis of the crucial significance of the French Revolution for the Romantics (pp. 26–72).

FURST, Lilian R., *Romanticism in Perspective*. London: Macmillan, 1969.
A comparative study of aspects of the Romantic movements in England, France and Germany that analyses differences as well as similarities.

GLECKNER, Robert F. & ENSCOE, Gerald E. (eds.), *Romanticism. Points of View*. 2nd ed. Englewood Cliffs, N. J.: Prentice-Hall, 1970.
Very useful collection of critical essays representing chief debates among scholars.

HALSTED, John B. (ed.), *Romanticism: Definition, Explanation and Evaluation* (Problems in European Civilization series). Boston: Heath, 1965.
Excerpts from Babbitt, Barzun, Croce, Foakes, Lovejoy, Wellek, etc. with brief introductory comments.

HUGO, Howard E. (ed.), *The Portable Romantic Reader. The Age of Romanticism (1756–1848) Mirrored in Poetry and Prose from England, France, Germany, and America.* New York: The Viking Press, 1957.
A large and convenient anthology, wide in interpretation of 'Romantic'.

POWELL, Annie E., *The Romantic Theory of Poetry.* London: Arnold, 1926.
A complex study with flashes of great insight.

'Romanticism: a Symposium', *Publications of the Modern Languages Association of America*, 55 (1940), pp. 1–60.
A set of brief articles on Romanticism in England, France, Germany, Italy and Spain; the quickest introduction to the whole field.

THORLBY, Anthony K. (ed.), *The Romantic Movement* (Problems and Perspectives in History series). London: Longman, 1966.
A linked series of extracts from various critics representing differing approaches and evaluations.

VAN TIEGHEM, Paul, *Le Romantisme dans la littérature européenne.* Paris: Michel, 1948.
A sweeping survey of Romanticism in European literature arranged according to themes and genres and seeking to synthesize similarities. Vast, though at times inaccurate, bibliography.

VAN TIEGHEM, Paul, *Ossian et l'Ossianisme dans la littérature européenne au XVIIIième siècle.* Groningen: Wolters, 1920.

Full of information on the staggering vogue for Ossian throughout Europe.

VAN TIEGHEM, Paul, *La Poésie de la nuit et des tombeaux*. Paris: Rieder, 1921.
An investigation of the melancholy aspect of Pre-Romanticism.

WELLEK, René, *A History of Modern Criticism*. Vol. i: *The Late Eighteenth Century*. Vol. ii: *The Romantic Age*. New Haven: Yale Univ. Press, 1955.
An indispensable survey of the evolution of ideas.

WELLEK, René, 'German and English Romanticism', in *Confrontations*. Princeton: Princeton Univ. Press, 1965, pp. 3–33.
Posits fundamental similarity and concedes certain differences.

English Romanticism

ABRAMS, Meyer H. (ed.), *English Romantic Poets: Modern Essays in Criticism*. New York: Oxford Univ. Press, 1960.
Reprints of some of the most rewarding essays in this field.

BERNBAUM, Ernest, *Guide through the Romantic Movement*. New York: Ronald Press, 1949.
Less of a guide than a collection of essays on individual English poets and on certain topics; full bibliographies.

FOAKES, Reginald A., *The Romantic Assertion*. London: Methuen, 1958.
An examination of the language of poetry with special attention to two structural images: the journey of life and the vision of love.

FORD, Boris (ed.), *From Blake to Byron*. Pelican Guide to English Literature, 5. Harmondsworth: Penguin Books, 1957.
Useful essays and bibliographies.

GERARD, Albert, *English Romantic Poetry*. Berkeley: Univ. of California Press, 1968.
An interpretation based on a most subtle analysis of certain poems.

HERFORD, Charles H., *The Age of Wordsworth*. London: Bell, 1914.
Though rather old-fashioned, still quite a sound account.

HILLES, Frederick W. & BLOOM, Harold (eds.), *From Sensibility to Romanticism. Essays Presented to Frederick A. Pottle*. New York: Oxford Univ. Press, 1965.
Worthwhile essays by eminent scholars on various facets of this period.

HOUGH, Graham, *The Romantic Poets*. London: Hutchinson's University Library, 1953.
A good basic study.

RODWAY, Alan, *The Romantic Conflict*. London: Chatto & Windus, 1963.
An original sociological interpretation.

French Romanticism

AFFRON, Charles, *A Stage for Poets. Studies in the Theatre of Hugo and Musset*. Princeton: Princeton Univ. Press, 1971.

BRAY, René, *Chronologie du romantisme*. Paris: Boivin, 1932.
Day-by-day, blow-by-blow account of the emergence of the Romantic movement in France.

MICHAUD, Guy & VAN TIEGHEM, Philippe, *Le Romantisme*. Paris: Hachette, 1952.
Rather schematic in its use of diagrams and perhaps over-simplified, but basically a very sound portrayal of the Romantic movement in France.

PEYRE, Henri, *Qu'est-ce que le romantisme?* Paris: Presses Universitaires, 1971.
A fairly conventional account.

TRAHARD, Pierre, *Le Romantisme défini par Le Globe*. Paris: Presses françaises, 1924.
A well-illustrated outline of shifts of opinion in France during the emergence of the Romantic movement.

VAN TIEGHEM, Philippe, *Le Romantisme français*. 5th ed. Paris: Presses Universitaires, 1957.
A good introduction.

VIAL, Francisque & DENISE, Louis, *Idées et doctrines littéraires du XVIIIième siècle*. Paris: Delagrave, 1930.
VIAL, Francisque & DENISE, Louis, *Idées et doctrines littéraires du XIXième siècle*. Paris: Delagrave, 1937.
Convenient compilations of texts from various journals and treatises.

German Romanticism

KORFF, H. A., *Geist der Goethezeit*. 5 vols. Leipzig: Koehler & Amelang, 1949–58.
This penetrating, highly illuminating work is, unfortunately, available only in German.

MASON, Gabriel R., *From Gottsched to Hebbel*. London: Harrap, 1961.
A useful, if elementary, introduction to this period of German literature.

PRAWER, Siegbert (ed.), *The Romantic Period in Germany*. London: Weidenfield & Nicolson, 1970.
Collection of essays by diverse scholars, mostly of high standard and covering Philosophy, Music, Aphorism, Romanticism and the German Language, as well as Drama, Lyric, *Märchen*, etc.

STENZEL, Gerhard (ed.), *Die deutschen Romantiker*. 2 vols. Salzburg: Bergland, n.d.
A comprehensive and very well presented anthology of texts with introduction, chronological tables, map and illustrations.

TAYLOR, Ronald, *The Romantic Tradition in Germany. An Anthology*. London: Methuen, 1970.
Excerpts, with introductions and commentaries, from the works of Herder, Wackenroder, Fichte, Novalis, Fr. Schlegel, Schopenhauer and R. Wagner.

TYMMS, Ralph, *German Romantic Literature*. London: Methuen, 1955.
A comprehensive but not always felicitous account.

WILLOUGHBY, Leonard A., *The Romantic Movement in Germany*. London: Oxford Univ. Press, 1930.
A handy brief summary.

Spanish Romanticism

KING, Edmund L., 'What is Spanish Romanticism?' *Studies in Romanticism*, 2 (1962), pp. 1–11.
How and why Spanish Romanticism differs from that of other countries.

PEERS, Edgar Allison, *A History of the Romantic Movement in Spain*. Cambridge: Cambridge Univ. Press, 1940.
The standard account of Spanish Romanticism.

SHAW, D. L., 'Towards the Understanding of Spanish Romanticism', *Modern Language Review*, 58 (1963), pp. 190–5. Emphasizes the need to take the ideological aspects into account.

TARR, F. Courtney, 'Romanticism in Spain and Spanish Romanticism: A Critical Survey', *Bulletin of Spanish Studies*,16 (1939), pp. 3–37.
A useful brief synthesis.

Italian Romanticism

DONADONI, Eugenio, *A History of Italian Literature*. Translated by Richard Monges. New York: New York Univ. Press, 1969.
A convenient brief overview.

FUBINI, Mario, *Romanticismo italiano*. 3rd. ed. Bari: Laterza, 1965.
The authoritative work, available only in Italian.

HAZARD, Paul, 'Le romantisme italien dans ses rapports avec le romantisme européen', *Revue de Littérature comparée*, 6, No. 2 (1926), pp. 224–45.
An attempt to place Italian Romanticism in the European framework.

Music and art

CHANTAVOINE, Jean & GAUDEFROY-DEMOMBYNES, Jean, *Le Romantisme dans la musique européenne*. Paris: Michel, 1955.

CLARK, Kenneth, *The Romantic Rebellion*. London & New York: Harper & Row, 1973.
A finely illustrated analysis of the differences between Romantic and Classic art.

Einstein, Alfred, *Music in the Romantic Era*. New York: Norton, 1947.
Informative without being too technical.

Newton, Eric, *The Romantic Rebellion*. New York: St. Martin's Press, 1962.
A stimulating and far-ranging analysis of the meaning of Romanticism in the visual arts.

Quennell, Peter, *Romantic England: Writing and Painting 1717–1851*. London: Weidenfeld & Nicolson, 1970.
Imaginative and beautifully illustrated enquiry into such topics as 'The Gothic Background', 'The Cult of Youth', 'The Earthly Paradise', etc.

The Romantic Movement. Catalogue of the 1959 Exhibition at the Tate Gallery, London. London: Arts Council of Great Britain, 1959.
A well-documented list with fine illustrations and thoughtful introductory essays on Romanticism in the graphic arts.

The aftermath

Adams, Robert M., *Nil. Episodes in the literary conquest of void during the nineteenth century*. New York: Oxford Univ. Press, 1966.
An original, intuitive book that opens up fresh perspectives.

Babbitt, Irving, *Rousseau and Romanticism*. Boston: Houghton Mifflin, 1919.
An eccentric and challenging disparagement of Romanticism and its consequences.

Béguin, Albert, *L'âme romantique et le rêve*. Paris: Corti, 1939.
A seminal work on the lineage from Romanticism towards Symbolism.

KERMODE, Frank, *Romantic Image*. London: Routledge, 1957.
A suggestive book, concerned mainly with the later Romantic generation of Yeats rather than with that of Wordsworth.

PECKHAM, Morse, *Beyond the Tragic Vision*. New York: Braziller, 1962.
An ingenious view of the nineteenth century as a period of reconstruction after the collapse of values.

PRAZ, Mario, *The Romantic Agony*. London: Oxford Univ. Press, 1933.
A fascinating and far-reaching book on the 'decadent' after-effects of Romanticism.

Index